MARTIN LUTHER
AND
THE REFORMATION

MARTIN LUTHER AND THE REFORMATION

C. T. Thomas

2012

Martin Luther and the Reformation – Published by the Rev. Dr. Ashish Amos of Indian Society for Promoting Christian Knowledge (ISPCK), Post Box 1585, 1654 Madarsa Road, Kashmere Gate, Delhi-110006.

© Author, 2012

All rights reserved. No part of this book may be reproduced or transmitted in any form or by any means, electronic, mechanical, photocopying, recording, or by any information storage and retrieval system, without the prior permission in writing from the publisher.

The views expressed in the book are those of the author and the publisher takes no responsibility for any of the statements.

Acknowledgements: Scripture quotations are taken from the Holy Bible, New International Version (NIV) Copyright 1973, 1978, 1984, International Bible Society. Used by permission of Zondervan Bible Publishers.

Due acknowledgement is made also for the following: New English Bible (NEB), New King James (NKJ), The Letters of the New Testament (NTL) and J. B. Phillips, The New Testament in Modern English (Phillips).

ISBN: 978-81-8465-230-7

Laser typeset by **ISPCK,** Post Box 1585,
1654 Madarsa Road, Kashmere Gate, Delhi-110006
Tel: 23866322, 23866323
e-mail–ashish@ispck.org.in   •   ella@ispck.org.in
website-www.ispck.org.

Dominus Illuminatio Mia

Contents

Dedication		v
Preface		ix
Chapter 1	Reformation and the Apostolic Church	1
Chapter 2	The Catholic Church and the Rise of the Papacy	10
Chapter 3	The Background of the Reformation	18
Chapter 4	The Life of Martin Luther	39
Chapter 5	Luther and the Bible: His Discovery of the Gospel	68
Chapter 6	Luther's Other Major Writings	75
Chapter 7	The English Reformation	94
Chapter 8	The Aftermath: Calvinists, Puritans and Dissidents	101
Chapter 9	Conclusion	114
Bibliography		118

PREFACE

On completion of my previous book *Behold the Man* (OM Authentic, 2006) I spent the next several months exploring various topics and themes for a viable subject of study and research. For one reason or another, after a good deal of reading and note-taking on each topic, all had to be abandoned as untenable. It was then that by a happy chance some of the primary works of Martin Luther fell into my hands. A perusal of these fired my imagination as none of the previous works I had consulted during the quest for a suitable topic had done, that then and there I resolved to take up the topic "Marin Luther and the Reformation" for serious study. The present work is the fruit of that study.

It did not take me long to realise that despite his mammoth achievement in radically shaking up the medieval Catholic Church, Luther's work was little understood and even his name was little known even among fairly well-educated friends and acquaintances of mine. There was a distinct tendency among them to get the early sixteenth-century Protestant reformer confused with the Civil Rights leader Martin Luther King Junior! "Aren't there two of them?" and "do you mean the father or the son?" were typical of some of the surprising responses that I received when I said that I was working on Martin Luther and the Reformation. This general apathy and relative ignorance no doubt acted as a stimulus to press on with the work. Although I was rather well acquainted in a general way with the work of Luther in relation to the history of Christianity, to my great joy I discovered that I had providentially stumbled upon a pearl of great price in some of the original works of Luther. Perusing some of the primary works of Luther, in particular the Prefaces to the several books of the Luther Bible and his lectures on them, as indeed researching the entire field, was a great learning experience for me. It did not take me long to arrive at the conclusion that no one had so deeply delved into the mystery of the Gospel nor brought out and communicated it with such lucidity and simplicity as he had done. After a close study of the primary works I venture to assert that few scholars and students of the Bible can match Luther in his knowledge and understanding of God's Word and fewer still who can expound its mysteries and insights as lucidly, simply and effectively as he has been able to do. I must confess in all humility that there is much more to learn, "had we but world enough and time" because, may be, I have touched only on the fringes of this enormous topic. But already "at my back I ...hear time's winged chariot hurrying near." Moreover there is the irresistible lure of "fresh woods, and pastures new." It was but natural that when the project was finished that I should want to give the reading public the benefit of my labours. I enjoyed researching the topic and writing it up as both tasks were a sheer labour of love. Needless to add, I do hope and pray that the reader will derive as much enjoyment in reading it as I had in writing it.

Chapter 1

REFORMATION AND THE APOSTOLIC CHURCH

If we are asked to name the principal benefactors of mankind or men who helped to change the world of their times, it is rarely, if ever, that Martin Luther would figure on the list. There is an odd chance that the Civil Rights crusader Martin Luther King would take precedence of the doughty champion of the Reformation. Yet by his intrepid personal courage, his unflinching belief in the justice of his cause and his unshakable trust in God, Luther took on the task of sweeping clean the most powerful institution in medieval Europe, namely the Catholic Church. Through the Reformation that he spearheaded, this rather nondescript and obscure little German monk became the agent of the transformation of Europe from the penumbra of medievalism to the light of modern times. To realize somewhat the enormous magnitude of his achievement, we have only to picture for a moment a Europe sans Luther. By boldly challenging assumptions long held inviolate and sacrosanct, Luther helped to release a mass of liberating human energies that positively impacted upon European ethos for generations to come. Heeding the wise counsel of Aristotle that a clear definition of terms is a prerequisite to all rational inquiry, let us open our discourse with two key definitions.

Reformation: 1. Improvement in form or quality; alteration to a better form; correction or removal of faults or errors; rebuilding. b. Improvement in health. Johnson. 2. Improvement of (or in) an existing state of things, institution, practice, etc.; a radical change for the better effected in political, religious, or social affairs 1460. b. *spec.* (with capital). The great religious movement of the 16th century, having for its object the reform of the doctrines and practices of the Church of Rome, and ending in the establishment of the various Reformed or Protestant Churches of central and north-western Europe 1563. 3. The action of reforming (one's own or another's) conduct or morals; improvement or amendment in this respect; correction 1509.

Re-formation: The action of forming again; a second or new formation.

The foregoing citation from the *Shorter Oxford English Dictionary* (SOED) which forms part of the definition of the terms Reformation and Re-formation points to their enormous complexity. Although we justifiably associate the great religious movement called the Reformation with events that happened in Europe in the sixteenth century, its roots lie as far back as the apostolic Church of the first century of the Christian era. As a matter of fact, reformation had its origin in the ministry of Jesus of Nazareth. Jesus, by His life, teaching and His unique insights into Judaism, had, in a sense, wrought a re-formation and a genuine reformation of the ancient faith of the Hebrews. He replaced the ancient Jewish covenant based on the Mosaic Law with His new covenant based on love. The reformation that Jesus initiated is both a reformation and a renaissance — both a re-formation and re-nascence or re-birth. Christianity is, *ipso facto,* a reform movement. As Jesus clarified in His colloquy with Nicodemus, the first step in the process is a new birth for each and every follower of Jesus Christ. The Church of Christ is a community of regenerated individuals. Jesus came to make all things new. "Behold, I make all things new" (Revelation 21:4). Here is how Paul envisions the Church of Jesus Christ. Addressing the Christian community in Ephesus he says:

> Thus you are no longer aliens in a foreign land, but fellow-citizens with God's people, members of God's household. You are built upon the foundation laid by apostles and prophets, and Christ himself is the foundation-stone. In him the whole building is bonded together and grows into a holy temple in the Lord.
> (Ephesians 2: 20-21; NEB)

All attempts at reform are in a way a harking back to the past, to a golden age that is the ideal of every attempt to re-build a Holy, Catholic and Apostolic Church. Therefore in order to trace the history of the Reformation we are constrained to look at the young Church in action in the very first century of the Christian calendar. To our great good fortune in The Acts of the Apostles we do possess an invaluable document dealing with an incipient Christian community. In Luke,[1] its author—he is the founding-father of ecclesiastical history as well as the author of the third Gospel— we have a historian of impeccable credentials and integrity. What does this document tell us of the salient character of the tiny burgeoning community of Jesus' disciples and associates?

Evangelist Luke gives us a lucid, though succinct, account of the fledgling community's corporate life in a classic statement that is hard to improve upon:

> They [the first converts] devoted themselves in close fellowship to instruction from the Apostles, to regular Breaking of Bread and to prayer. The Apostles performed many miracles and wonders, and a feeling of awe came over every soul. They lived as a community and shared everything; they sold their property and belongings and distributed the money among themselves according to need. Every day they met in the Temple in unity of spirit, broke bread together in each other's houses, took their food with glad and simple hearts, and gave praise to God. They enjoyed the goodwill of the Jewish people, and the Lord increased their community daily by new converts.[2]

Curiously enough I find an echo of Luke's narrative in the account that the Jewish historian Josephus gives of the Jewish sect called the Essenes.

---

[1] Hailed by Paul as "the beloved physician," Luke was, by profession, a physician from Antioch. For some time he was a companion and personal physician attending on Paul. We encounter him as Paul's sole companion as he lay languishing in a dungeon during his second incarceration in Nero's Rome. What is clear from his writings is that he is a highly educated man of wide culture. His Greek, as well as his sense of style, is superior to that of the other New Testament writers.

[2] Acts 2: 42-47 (Saint Luke: *The Acts of the Apostles*, Tr. C. H. Rieu; Penguin Classics, 1957).

> These men [the Essenes] are despisers of riches, and so very communicative [affectionate, friendly] as raises our admiration. Nor is there any one to be found among them who hath more than another; for it is a law among them, that those who come to them must let what they have be common to the whole order, in so much, that among them all there is no appearance of poverty nor excess of riches, but every one's possessions are intermingled with every other's possessions: and so there is, as it were, one patrimony among all the brethren.[3]

In Luke's depiction of the Apostolic Church we witness a cohesion and symbiosis rarely if ever encountered in any human corporation. For the first time in human history we are witnessing genuine Christian fellowship in action. The love and faith which infused them would be the most outstanding characteristic that would strike an external observer. After Jesus' resurrection and the repeated appearances which many of them had witnessed, they were now convinced that their erstwhile teacher and boon companion was none other than the Christ of God. What we do get from Luke's history is a picture of genuine, authentic Christianity in dynamic action, as its founder intended that it should be practised and lived by. Here is a group of quite ordinary men and women who have been brought together by their single-minded devotion to their departed Master who, they believed, was now alive and living in glory. There is an overwhelming quality of oneness that binds together this tiny community of Christians. The whole group is imbued with an air of rare Christian love, care and fellowship. What is this mysterious and mystical bond that binds them all together? Here is a tiny community of quite ordinary men and women, without silver or gold, power or prestige, setting forth courageously to conquer the pagan world for Christ with the message of universal love and brotherhood.

Since the Apostolic times there have been numerous attempts to recreate the pristine purity and simplicity and extra-ordinary fellowship of first-century Christianity, but

---

[3] Flavius Josephus, *The Wars of the Jews*, Book II, Chapter VIII, Section iii.

we are yet to witness a single one that has been an unqualified success. Even the best-laid plans soon get entangled and lost in the labyrinth of hierarchy and institutionalism. Nevertheless, the yearning to recapture the spirit of the early Christian brotherhood is an ideal that refuses to be extinguished. It is perhaps simply beyond human capacity to create the unique fellowship of the small Christian community in today's world-wide Church. But nothing is beyond the power of Almighty God. All shall turn out well in His good time.

The picture that we looked at of the post-Pentecostal community may have continued intact only for a limited time. The sharing of worldly goods and daily worship in the Temple courts could not have gone on for long. With the Good News being accepted by the Gentiles and the subsequent growth of the community beyond the pale of Palestine, changes must inevitably have come about. It may be an interesting and profitable exercise to try and build a profile of an early house-church and visualise a typical service on the Lord's Day, as post-Resurrection Sunday came to be called. The template that the Apostles had for a house-church was most likely the Jewish synagogue with appropriate adjustments and modifications. The New Testament furnishes only scanty evidence on which to build a profile of divine worship in a primitive church. One invariable communal act in which all believers experienced a spiritual union must, indeed, have been in the Breaking of Bread. This hallowed memorial to Jesus' supreme sacrifice must have formed the heart of the divine service. We may gain at least some faint inkling into the extraordinary fellowship that existed in the early Christian communities and the rare mystique that they associated with the Breaking of the Bread from the following:

> The cup of blessing which we bless, is it not the communion of the blood of Christ? The bread which we break, is it not the communion of the body of Christ? For we being many are one bread, and one body: for we are all partakers of that one bread. (1 Corinthians 10: 16-17).

But as Paul's letter to the community at Corinth reveals, it did not take long for the sacrament to lose some of its earlier purity and sanctity. In it we find Paul exhorting the congregation to observe the ceremony with due diligence and propriety.[4] Readings from the Scriptures, i.e., The Old Testament, must have formed part of church worship as the early Christians had access only to the Jewish Bible. It is reasonable to assume that the worshippers would have chosen to read portions out of the Messianic prophecies. From the recorded addresses of Peter and Paul in Acts, we may safely infer that the theme of the sermons in all likelihood would have been their witness that Jesus of Nazareth, whom the Jews in their arrogance and ignorance had cruelly done to death by nailing Him on the cross, was indeed their long-awaited Messiah. Prayers, prophecies and speaking in tongues, are a few other activities that find mention in Paul's letters.

> When you meet together, one of you will have a psalm, another a teaching, another a revelation from God, another will speak in tongues, another will have an interpretation of what is spoken. But everything that is done must help the church. Two of you, or at the most three, may speak in tongues, each in turn, and someone must interpret. However, if there is no one to interpret, they must be silent in the assembly. Let them speak to themselves and to God. In the same way, two or three prophets may speak, and the others should weigh carefully what is said. But if someone who is sitting in the meeting receives a revelation, the first speaker should stop. In this way you can all prophecy one by one, so that everyone may learn and be encouraged. For the spirits of prophets are under the control of the prophets, and God is not a God of confusion but of peace.[5]

Regarding church administration and its various offices too we do get but scant evidence from the Acts and the Epistles. Foremost among all its services, apart from the preaching of the Word, was almsgiving and the distribution of charity to the needy, especially to the widows among them. It is significant that the first office to receive mention

---

[4] 1 Corinthians 11: 20-34.

[5] 1 Corinthians 14: 26-33, *The Letters of the New Testament*, The New Translation (Tyndale House Publishers, 1990).

in Acts was that of deacons[6] who were picked from among the believers to distribute alms equitably. We read that the first deacons were chosen so that the Apostles could devote themselves to prayer and the proclamation of the Gospel. A three-fold criterion determined the selection of deacons, namely, good reputation, conspicuous wisdom and fullness of the Holy Spirit. Their ordination was marked by the absence of any elaborate ceremony. The narrative in Acts makes it clear that it consisted solely of prayer and the laying on of the Apostle's hands. Other leadership offices that find mention are elders or bishops.[7] It would appear that the words bishop, elder and overseer were used interchangeably as all of them refer to similar, if not identical functions. However, while 'elder' indicates qualifications such as maturity and experience, in 'overseer' the stress is on the responsibility of looking after God's people. Paul has given us a rather detailed list of the requisite qualifications for a prospective bishop or elder — or, more properly, an overseer — and deacon.[8] This was imparted to two very young 'elders' Titus and Timothy who had been given the responsibility of ministering to two incipient congregations in Crete and Ephesus respectively. In view of their comparative youth — Timothy, in particular must have been very young — doubts have been expressed whether they can really be designated overseers. But the point is that they were carrying out the duties and functions proper to that office, whether they were officially designated as such or

---

[6] 'Deacon' comes from the Greek word used to describe the function of the office, i.e., to wait on at tables. 'Deacon' can also mean minister or servant (See note to Acts 6: 6 in NIV Study Bible). Deacons were first selected in order to distribute alms to the poor and destitute widows — that is, as Almoners — in the Christian community in Jerusalem. Stephen, the first Christian martyr, was among the seven deacons or almoners chosen at that time.

[7] Different translations of the Bible use different terms such as bishop, overseer or elder. They are translations of the Greek *episcopos* which literally means an overseer.

[8] I Timothy 3: 1-13; Titus 2: 5-9.

not. In Judaism one had to be thirty years old to be a member of the Sanhedrin or supreme Jewish Council. The same criterion may have applied to be a governor of a synagogue. The same or similar consideration may have guided the apostles in naming overseers. A formidable array of accomplishments and virtues were sought for in a prospective candidate for the office of an elder. The following is only part of the qualities and qualifications needed.

> Our leader, therefore, or bishop, must be above reproach, faithful to his one wife, sober, temperate, courteous, hospitable, and a good teacher; he must not be given to drink, or a brawler, but of a forbearing disposition, avoiding quarrels, and no lover of money. He must be one who manages his own household well and wins obedience from his children, and a man of the highest principles. If a man does not know how to control his own family, how can he look after a congregation of God's people? (1 Timothy 2: 2-5; NEB)

Apparently elders were held in high regard and great reverence as evidenced by Peter and John, the chief among the disciples and apostles of Jesus, content to be called elders (I Peter 5:1; I & II John). In the same context Peter exhorts elders to shepherd their flocks, not by constraint, but willingly looking up to the pattern set by the Great Shepherd who laid down His life for the sake of the sheep. Already there might have been stray cases of church offices being misused for making dishonest gain from Peter's warning to elders to perform their duties eagerly not with an eye to gainful employment.[9] All these qualities and many more were required to be a leader besides a firm grounding in sound Christian doctrine. The qualities and qualifications needed to become a deacon were equally onerous. Interestingly, bishops and deacons being older men, Paul seems to assume that they must be married men with wife and children. However, presumably an unmarried man was not barred from holding either position.[10] Paul's careful eye

---

[9] I Peter 5: 1-4.

[10] Please see NIV Study Bible for tabulated statement of the respective qualities called for to be an overseer or deacon.

does not fail to mention the need to give the pastors adequate emoluments as a legitimate charge on the church. On the whole, the profile of the Apostolic Church that emerges from the New Testament, the Epistles of Paul, for instance, is one of absolute purity and holiness, if she is worthy to be the undefiled Bride of the Lamb. From a perusal of the foregoing far-from-complete narrative of the first-century Christian congregation's religious service and church administration, it would become abundantly clear that we today have departed markedly from the original pattern. How far the old dispensation ought to be brought back and how practical is it to do so are certainly moot points to ponder.

Despite being called the Acts of the Apostles,[11] neither Peter nor John, nor even Paul, on whom its author devotes more attention and space than the other two, is the prime mover in Luke's story. The principal protagonist in this first act of the Christian drama of redemption is not a human agent at all. It is indeed the Holy Spirit. After spending several months in close study of this remarkable book, here is the testimony of one of its modern translators: "No one can read this book without being convinced that there is *Someone* here at work besides mere human beings."[12] Having been imbued with the Holy Spirit at Pentecost in fulfillment of the Master's pledge to them, Peter and John and their companions are now no longer the simple fishermen or ordinary country folk that they used to be. They have been fully transformed, metamorphosed from the cowering mice that they were when their Master was ignominiously done to death by being nailed to the cross, to the fearless lions of the post-resurrection days, ready to dare the high and mighty of the land. The secret of this fearless force was that each and every word and action of the tiny community was dictated to and overseen by the Holy Spirit.

---

[11] A literal translation of the title in Greek would read either, Acts of Apostles (without the definite article) or Some Acts of Some Apostles.

[12] J. B. Phillips, *The Young Church in Action* (London: Bles, 1955).

Chapter 2

THE CATHOLIC CHURCH AND THE RISE OF THE PAPACY

Despite the ordeal of the fire of persecution through which the fledgling Christian community has had to pass, owing to the overwhelming divine grace it enjoyed, instead of withering and perishing, it was able to withstand even imperial hostility and sustain a robust growth. Before long it managed to win over numerous adherents among the emperor's legions and even succeeded in penetrating Caesar's household and finally permeated the length and breadth of the vast Roman Empire. The fortunes of the Church underwent a climactic transformation with the dramatic conversion of the Emperor Constantine (272-337; Emperor 306-337). The story of his conversion reads almost like a fairytale. Legend has it that during his campaign against Maxentius in 312, he saw a luminous cross of Christ on the imperial standard and inscribed on it the insignia *in hoc signo vinces* (in this sign [you will] conquer) and evinced the same insignia and motto on the shields of his soldiers. He defeated Maxentius near Rome, embraced Christianity and so became the first Christian emperor. By the Edict of Milan (313), Christianity, which in earlier times suffered the opprobrium of being regarded as an illicit and illegal sect, at last received royal approbation as a legal entity along with Rome's pagan cults. Constantine also gifted the Lateran Palace in Rome for the residence of the bishop of Rome. Moreover he declared Sunday as a day of worship, encouraged the construction of places for Christians to worship and extended patronage to the copying and production of copies of the Bible. It was during his tenure that the construction of old St. Peter's began. The status and prestige of the Church underwent a sea change under the sustained patronage it received during the reign of Theodosius the Great (379-395). After receiving the sacrament of baptism, in a solemn edict, among other provisions, he forbade the worship of pagan cults and religions. By royal edict, pagan temples and idols were destroyed and sacrifices were prohibited and declared as criminal acts. Christianity was proclaimed the state religion and Sunday was declared a holiday. By the same edict he authorised the followers of Christ "to assume the title of Catholic Christians".[1] At long last the Galilean[2] seemed to have won His ultimate triumph! Yet ironically, the spiritual decadence of the Church coincided with the moment of its apparent triumph when Christianity, instead of being hunted and hounded by the agents of imperial Rome found patronage and protection under the wings of the Roman Eagle.

Tracing the history and vicissitudes of the Church forms no part of this study. However, the birth, growth and the evolution of the papacy in Rome and its ascendancy to the primacy of the Catholic Church need to be looked at as they are relevant to our principal theme. The provenance of the Church in the imperial city of Rome remains a mystery. Extant evidence points to the presence of a Jewish community in the city at least from the second century B.C. During the Roman general Pompey's triumphal progress into the imperial capital in 61 B.C., after his conquest of Judea in 63 B.C., it is chronicled that many Jewish prisoners of war graced the

---

[1] Detailed provisions of the edict can be read in Edward Gibbon, *The Decline and Fall of the Roman Empire*, Volume III, p.86.

[2] *Vicisti Galilaee* ("Thou hast conquered, O Galilean"). These were the dying words of the Emperor Julian (331-363), commonly called Julian the Apostate, after he received his death wound from a Christian. Julian, brought up as a Christian, renounced the faith and went back to pagan worship on becoming emperor. Julian's sentiments are echoed in A. C. Swinburne's poem "Hymn to Proserpine." 'Wilt thou take all, Galilean . . . Thou hast conquered, O pale Galilean; the world has grown grey from thy breath.'

procession. In Jerusalem during the historic Pentecost when the Holy Spirit was poured down on the disciples, there were present "visitors from Rome, both Jews and proselytes" (Acts 2: 10; NEB). Could a few of the newly converted Christians have constituted the nucleus of the Roman congregation? In his book *The Twelve Caesars* the Roman historian and biographer Suetonius (c. A.D. 55-c. A.D. 117) says that in A.D. 41 Claudius Caesar expelled Jews from Jerusalem because they constantly created disturbance at the instigation of *Chrestus*. It has been plausibly conjectured that *Chrestus* might be a reference to Christians because in the early days many considered Christianity to be a faction or sect within Judaism. By the time Paul wrote to Rome's Christians (56-57) he was clearly addressing a robust community with a preponderance of Gentile converts. His first visit to the imperial city in early 60 was not as a privileged Roman citizen as he had hoped and planned, but in a far different state as a prisoner in chains. From what we have said what can be asserted incontrovertibly is that Paul was not the founder of the Church in the imperial capital. Neither does it logically follow that since Paul was not the founder, Peter must have established the Roman Church. However, there is a hard-to-be-refuted tradition going back to the early days of Christianity that both Peter and Paul perished there during the insane persecution unleashed by the Roman Emperor Nero. Like the genesis of the church in Rome, the origin of the papacy, the prelacy of Rome, too is shrouded in mystery and the claim of the Roman Catholic Church that the Pope—derived from the Latin *pappas* and ecclesiastical Latin *papas* and *papa*, Italian for father—the bishop of Rome, is the apostolic successor to Peter and that, flowing from it, he is the Vicar[3] of Christ, is not based on solid evidence.

---

[3] As used in this context the title is quite a loaded one. 'Vicar' comes from *vicarius* (Latin), a substitute; a deputy. The title clearly implies that the Pope is the putative deputy of Christ on the earth.

THE CATHOLIC CHURCH AND THE RISE OF THE PAPACY

In early Christianity, besides Rome, the patriarchates of Antioch, Alexandria, Constantinople and Jerusalem also were reckoned pre-eminent. It would appear that in the beginning all Western bishops were accorded the title pope or papa. But by A.D. 500 it began to be restricted to the bishop of Rome based on the Catholic Church's claim to apostolic succession. However, the claim for supremacy by the bishop of Rome among the ancient archdioceses was summarily rejected as untenable by most of his compeers from very early days. After the division of the Empire in A.D. 395 into the Eastern Roman Empire with its capital in Constantinople and the Western Empire based in Rome, the Patriarchs of Antioch, Alexandria and Jerusalem gradually accepted the leadership of Constantinople. Thereafter there developed a rivalry between Rome and Constantinople for supremacy in Christendom. The final schism between East and West, between Constantinople and Rome, happened at the last Ecumenical Council held at Constantinople in A.D. 869. After the schism the Roman and the Greek Churches held separate councils. The Greek Orthodox Church of the East completely broke away from the Catholic Church. In a domain where Christ-like humility and Christian charity should preponderate, it is hardly edifying to see the followers of Jesus who put love above all values, fighting for dominion like some power-hungry secular rulers. Be that as it may, I suppose at the present time, the papacy and its claim to be supreme head of the world-wide Roman Catholic Church, and not simply the head of the bishopric of Rome, is widely accepted, believed by the Catholic faithful and tacitly tolerated by the people at large.

Despite the controversy regarding the Pope's supremacy over the other primates, the primacy of Peter among the apostles rests on much surer ground and has clear Biblical warranty in Jesus' commission:

> "And I tell you that you are Peter, and on this rock I will build my Church and the gates of Hades will not overcome it. I will give you the keys of the kingdom of heaven; whatever you bind on earth will be bound in heaven, and whatever you loose on earth will be loosed in heaven (Matthew 16: 18-19; NIV).

It was further confirmed by the risen Lord's three-fold injunction to Peter to feed His flock (John 21: 15-17). As has already been hinted, paradoxical as it may sound, it nevertheless remains true, that the spiritual decline of the Church began when it was brought under Roman imperial protection and patronage. Ironically, the Church had its periods of robust growth when it was subjected to persecution by the Roman emperors and its saints were tortured and killed in the most appalling and heinous ways imaginable. Simultaneously with the roster of its martyrs growing longer and bulkier, the Church extended its spatial sweep and grew in spiritual power. This truth is echoed in Tertullian's proverbial statement: "The blood of the martyrs is the seed of the Church." The early Church, it would seem, had paid good heed to Jesus' categorical affirmation at His trial before Pilate that His kingdom is not of this world. But with its adoption by the state, the Christian religion began to don the mantle of a martial and imperial power with all its attendant trappings and regalia. Gone were the days when the Holy Spirit directed its destiny in the first three centuries of its history. It was increasingly losing its spiritual power and was becoming more and more a secular, mundane, temporal and largely political establishment.

It is difficult to pin-point the exact time in which medieval papacy came into being. Its origin can be traced to Damasus I (366-384). It was he who decreed that the bishop of Rome was the direct successor of Apostle Peter and that therefore he was the true pope. Subsequently several successive popes in the next few centuries have attempted to embellish and enrich both the spiritual and temporal power of the office. Leo I (440-461) claimed that the pope's ex-cathedra pronouncements were of equal validity as Peter's own words. Meanwhile, political developments in the empire and in the city of Rome in particular further served the enhancement of papal power. With the diminution of the empire's power and influence in the wake of repeated barbarian invasions, the pope was often called upon to intervene in temporal affairs. Moreover the Catholic Church's propinquity to the empire's great metropolis naturally gave it a prominence vis-a-vis the other sees. Inevitably this factor eventually resulted in its unexcelled pre-eminence. Notwithstanding the earlier developments under Damasus I and Leo I already noted, Pope Gregory I, called the Great (590-604), is credited as the real founder of the medieval papacy. His genealogical descent from a wealthy noble family in Rome, his participation in Rome's administrative apparatus early in his career—he had been prefect of Rome—considerably enhanced the prestige of the papacy. It naturally resulted in his bringing into the Church many of the tinsel trappings of Rome's officialdom. His services to the Church were numerous and wide-ranging and earned him the appellation 'Great'. He is the originator of the Gregorian chant and the author of the immensely influential work in Latin—the language of the Catholic Church—*Cura Pastoralis* (Pastoral Care). It was he who despatched Augustine—of Canterbury in order that we may not confuse him with Augustine of Hippo—which resulted in the conversion of Anglo-Saxon England to Christianity.

In the chaotic political situation prevailing in many parts of Europe at the time, in 756 the emperor of the Eastern Roman Empire based in Constantinople sought the assistance of Pepin III, the king of the Franks, to drive out the marauding Lombards from the city of Ravenna. After a successful operation, instead of handing over the conquered territories to its rightful claimant the emperor, he handed them over to Pope Stephen II. This so called 'Donation of Pepin' laid the foundation of the papal state consisting of large areas of central Italy which the Roman Church ruled until its incorporation in 1870 into the newly-formed kingdom of Italy. As could have been naturally anticipated with the pope combining within himself absolute spiritual authority and great political power, in course of time there developed a tussle called the investiture controversy between the temporal and spiritual authorities as to which entity held the real, i.e., the superior power. In the course of this struggle, often kings and emperors were forced to bow to papal supremacy. For instance on Christmas Day 800 in Constantinople Pope Leo III (795-816) crowned Charlemagne Holy Roman Emperor.

Meanwhile in addition to supreme spiritual suzerainty, the popes began to arrogate to themselves extensive temporal authority also. This was done on the basis of what is known as 'the Donation of Constantine'.[4] This infamous 'Donation' is based on a document purportedly written by Emperor Constantine by which he acceded to the papal see sovereignty over Rome, parts of Italy and the "islands of the sea". On the strength of this spurious document, medieval popes claimed complete temporal jurisdiction over the whole of Western Christendom. Later on in the eleventh century the plenitude of papal power was attained in the time of Hildebrand who ascended the throne of Peter as Pope Gregory VII (1073-1085). He pronounced that the pope's authority being divinely ordained and bestowed from above exceeded the power of all earthly rulers. It was during his tenure as pope that priestly celibacy was made mandatory. To cut the story short, since its modest inception, over several centuries, by incremental additions the papal court glittered and glowed far above the grandeur and splendour of any earthly prince or potentate. Perhaps medieval papacy assumed its greatest power in the time of Pope Innocent III (1198-1216) who is reported to have said that only God was above the pope. The Holy Roman Emperor and the kings of France and England were made to acknowledge their subservience to his spiritual authority. Arrogating to himself the title 'Vicar of Christ', he ensured the subordination of

---

[4] In 1440 the Italian humanist and critic Lorenzo (Laurentius in Latin) Valla (1407-57), by analyzing its style and content, proved that the document could not have been written in the fourth century and that the "Donation" was a forgery concocted centuries later.

all temporal power to the Catholic Church. During his tenure as pope, at the Fourth Lateran Council (1215), the dogma of transubstantiation received acceptance as the Catholic Church's official credo. He vigorously pursued the policy of persecuting heretics through the Inquisition and sponsored the Fourth Crusade.

The medieval Catholic Church, under successive popes over-reached itself not only in power and prestige but equally in venality and corruption. The bull *Unam Sanctum* (One Holy) of Boniface VIII (1294-1303) maintained that there is only 'one Holy Catholic and Apostolic Church' of which the Roman pontiff is the head and that there is neither forgiveness of sins nor salvation outside the Catholic Church. In 1343 Pope Clement VI declared via his bull *Unigenitus* that the merits of Christ are a treasury of indulgences, thus paving the way for the sale of indulgences. Thus slowly, but steadily over the centuries a number of self-serving popes by means of their self-aggrandizing policies had brought the papacy to an unassailable position. By the time of the Reformation for almost a millennium as the Church prospered materially, it had fallen pathetically in its moral standards and no longer shone as a spiritual beacon to sinful and suffering humankind. There was a crying need for change and reform and reformation on an unexpected and unprecedented scale was very much in the offing. In closing this part of the study, a word of moderation and caution seems appropriate in the interests of fair play. From this long litany of papal misdeeds it should not be presumed that the patriarchates remaining outside the Roman fold adorned themselves in vestments of exceptional holiness and purity. While there were exceptions in all centres of Christianity with a number of churchmen who brought glory to the Kingdom of God by the purity of their spiritual life, most men in the higher echelons of the ecclesiastical hierarchy whether in the Western or Eastern Church were driven by the passions of power and pelf. The Catholic Church was ripe for a purge and the Reformation was at hand with the much-needed cleansing.

Chapter 3

THE BACKGROUND OF THE REFORMATION

The world into which Martin Luther was born was Catholic Europe. Religion occupied the greater part of the lives of most ordinary people. The Church, its institutions in the form of the parish church, the monasteries, and the more imposing basilicas and cathedrals, towered over the petty dwellings of the common folk. In medieval Christendom, wherever one turned, one knocked into people whose life was bound up with the service of the Church either in its spiritual or temporal side. The village parson, a travelling monk, pardoner or summoner, were quite familiar sights. Not infrequently one might even run into the progress of a great ecclesiastic to the accompaniment of an impressive retinue. Occasionally one came across pilgrims either singly or in groups wending their way to one or the other of the holy shrines of saints and martyrs in quest of the holy one's blessing or in fulfillment of a vow for favours received. Indeed, the Church Universal made its ubiquitous presence in one's everyday existence. It is no exaggeration to state that from the initial sacrament of baptism to the final one of extreme unction, from the cradle to the grave, the Church dominated every phase of a Christian's life. With the evolution of the Catholic Church as a near-universal phenomenon in amplitude, power and wealth, alongside there grew much profiteering in the provision of its sacraments and services. In the prevailing atmosphere of widespread illiteracy and ignorance among vast swathes of its lay masses, there was an undue reliance on the spiritual benefits of pilgrimages, worship, amounting to idolatry, of sacred relics and belief in false doctrines. The infamous sale of indulgences was just the last straw that broke the camel's back. This desperate situation called for a latter day Martin-Luther-turned-Hercules to cleanse the system. Whether by a happy coincidence or by historical inevitability, at this juncture several factors, political, social, cultural and scientific, converged and worked in unison to precipitate and facilitate a radical transformation of European society.

By no means was Martin Luther the first person to try to rid the Church of financial corruption and doctrinal abuses which had crept into it in the course of the past several centuries. Indeed, he had a number of notable precursors, as for example John Wycliffe in England and John Huss of Bohemia.[1] To take a look at the views of these men as regards Christian faith and practice is to see how closely Luther's Reformation ideals were anticipated by these earlier reformers. Hailed as a Protestant before the full flowering of Protestantism, John Wycliffe was a vehement adversary of the pope and a strong assailant of certain extreme elements of Catholic dogma which he felt were inconsistent with Christ's teaching. Similarly he was highly critical of the many corrupt practices which had crept into the Medieval Church. Born in Richmond in Yorkshire, he spent most of his active life at Oxford where he lectured on philosophy and is said to have been master of Balliol College for some time. His views on religion and philosophy owed something to William of Ockham, but the bedrock of his faith and practice was the Bible so much so that he is deservedly honoured with the title *Doctor Evangelicus*. Wycliffe was chaplain to Edward III and in that capacity he was drawn into a defence of the king in his dispute with Rome regarding the payment of dues to the Curia. France had already set an example by repudiating the excessive financial cesses demanded by the Roman Church. Following France's defiant stand, when Pope Urban

---

[1] The Czech Republic is the present-day successor state to Bohemia.

V sought arrears to Rome which had accrued during the previous thirty years from King Edward III, the king coolly rejected the claim. There was widespread resentment in the country against Rome's avaricious impositions. Buoyed up by the prevailing popular anti-papal national sentiment, Wycliffe raised his voice to defend the sovereign's superior right against the Curia's excessive exactions. He persisted in his opposition to Rome by attacking the institution of endowments which he felt was the root of all evil in the Catholic Church and called upon the civil power to curb the Church's greed by attaching its extensive estates.

In the comparative liberal and democratic ethos prevalent at the medieval university, in academic lectures, debates and disputations, Wycliffe continued unhindered to propagate his anti-establishment and anti-papal views. Meanwhile with the election in 1378 of the 'anti-pope' Clement VII, he turned increasingly at odds with Rome. Building his arguments solidly on the teaching of Jesus and the Bible, he demonstrated how the Roman Church had subverted Biblical truth. His anti-papal and anti-clerical views—besides enjoying popular support at home—had a huge impact on European scholars. Wycliffe's ideas gained currency in central Europe through the teaching and writing of Jerome of Prague and John Huss.

While his lectures and earlier writing had all been in Latin, being addressed to scholars and peers in the religious and academic fraternity, in the latter part of his career he turned increasingly to writing in his native English. The crown of his achievement—and his chief title to fame and the gratefulness of posterity—remains his rendering of the Scriptures into the vernacular language. The Wycliffe Bible was the fruit of his conviction that to be ignorant of the Bible was to be ignorant of Christ and His teaching. Consequently he resolutely set his mind on turning the Bible into his native tongue. With the assistance of coadjutors the Scriptures were translated into English from the Latin

Vulgate. The Wycliffe English version was the first ever entire Bible to be published in any European vernacular. Despite his great achievements and his popularity among vast sections of his countrymen, owing to the radical nature of his religious views he was forced to leave Oxford. He lived out the remainder of his life in relative isolation and obscurity at Lutterworth where he was rector from 1374 to 1375. In an age intolerant of any deviation from the official ecclesiastical teaching, it still remains a mystery why Wycliffe's heterodox views did not invite the Church's extreme penalty. He had a natural end and was buried in the village churchyard. Yet the Church's deadly retribution would not leave his mortal remains alone. In 1428 his body was exhumed and burnt by order of a papal commission and his bones were cast into the river Swift. Here is how a later well-known English writer memorialises the sad fate meted out to one of the most outstanding of the pioneer-reformers of the Church and the very first translator of the Bible into English.

> They ordered his bones... to be taken out of the ground and thrown far off from any Christian burial... and cast into Swift, a neighbouring brook.... This brook conveyed his ashes into Avon, Avon into Severn, Severn into the narrow seas, they into the main Ocean. Thus the ashes of Wycliffe are the emblems of his doctrine, which is now dispersed all the world over.[2]

A name that naturally calls for honourable mention and brief discussion alongside Wycliffe's is that of the Czech patriot and reformer John Huss (Jan Hus in the Czech language). If Wycliffe is called the 'morning star' of the Reformation, Huss too deserves to be counted among the principal fore-runners of the reform movement. Born in Southern Bohemia in 1369, Huss studied at the University of Prague from which he obtained bachelor's degrees in arts as

---

[2] Thomas Fuller, *Church-History of Britain*. Thomas Fuller (1608-1661), English clergyman and writer, was chaplain to King Chares II. His best-known work is *The History of the Worthies of England* (1662), a collection of biographical sketches.

well as in theology, followed by a master's degree in arts. While at the university he came under the spell of Wycliffe, some of whose writings he translated into the Czech language. Inspired by the Englishman's ideas, he sought to propagate his views among his countrymen. In 1400 Huss was ordained a priest and two years later was made preacher at the Bethlehem Chapel—a foundation dedicated to preaching in the Czech language—in Prague. Apparently, the use of the people's language in preference to Latin, the language of the Church, was contrary to the precept and practice of the Catholic Church at the time. Nevertheless, because of the influence of Huss, the Bethlehem Church became a rallying point and a beacon for worshippers desirous of Church reform. His sermons in the language of the people gave rise to intense nationalistic sentiments throughout Bohemia and he became a national hero, an honour that he still enjoys among his countrymen. In his sermons he attacked the widespread corruption that was rampant at the time in the Catholic Church. His opposition to the granting of papal indulgences earned him many enemies in the Church's establishment. However, he enjoyed the protection and patronage of Emperor Wenceslaus IV who made him Rector of Prague University. Huss's attacks on the Church and the radical views of Wycliffe to which he gave wide currency alarmed the archbishop of Prague who complained to the pope. With the support of the pope, the archbishop forbade Huss to preach at the Bethlehem Chapel. When Wycliffe's books were publicly burned by the archbishop's orders, Huss vehemently protested. The retribution of the Church was swift to follow. The pope now excommunicated him. To save the city of Prague from a papal interdiction, Huss left the city and retired to a place called Tabor. In the two years he spent there in retirement he wrote all his important works including *De Ecclesia* (*The Church*), in which he denied the infallibility of the pope, affirmed the primacy of the Scriptures over man-made rules, and asserted the right of the state to reform the Church. He was now accused of heresy and ordered to appear before the Council of Constance. Although provided with a safe conduct by Emperor Sigusmund, on reaching Constance he found himself in incarceration and put on trial as a heretic. On his refusal to recant, he was burnt at the stake in 1415. His friend and fellow-worker Jerome of Prague too suffered the same fate. Interestingly, one finds numerous references to Huss in Luther's writings. He cites Huss's positive stand on infant baptism to reinforce his own belief that this sacrament as conducted by the Church from ancient times is sanctified as the ceremony is accompanied by the outpouring of the Holy Spirit. In *An Appeal to the Ruling Class* Luther makes an impassioned plea that the reform movement should align itself with the Hussites—as the followers of John Huss came to be called—as such a union would strengthen both sides.

Theologians and preachers such as Wycliffe and Huss were not alone in deprecating churchmen for their moral turpitude and greed for gain. Contemporary writers too were vehement in denouncing the widespread corruption current in the Church at the time. Among these Langland and Chaucer stand distinguished for their skilful exposure of ecclesiastical abuses. However, pride of place must go to Geoffrey Chaucer (1340-1400) for the urbane wit and suave good humour with which he manages his ironic— nevertheless devastatingly brutal—thrusts at his victims. Though ostensibly a work of fiction, contemporary social historians do attest to the realism and authenticity of his portraits in the *Canterbury Tales*. In the Prologue to the poem we meet a cavalcade of pilgrims—many of them ecclesiastical dignitaries—wending its way to the shrine in the Canterbury Cathedral of the martyred saint, Thomas Becket. A closer look at the characters will reveal the level of corruption and degradation to which the various orders of the Church had degenerated. The affluent atmosphere in which the inmates of monasteries and nunneries—who were wedded to chastity, poverty and obedience—lived in medieval England can be easily gauged from the sketches of Madame Eglantyn, a nun, and Dan Piers, her fellow pilgrim and a monk. In gross violation of rules the nun kept small dogs as pets and catered to their dainty palates by feeding them with fine quality wheaten bread and roast meats! The sad irony lay in the fact that while luxury reigned within members of the Church's orders which were ostensibly wedded to poverty, the poor peasants in the neighbourhood of these religious houses lived in abject indigence and deprivation! Dan Piers, the monk, lived in total disregard of his monastic vows. A glutton and a pleasure seeker, his favourite pastime was hunting, a forbidden pastime to monks who were committed by their monastic vows to lead cloistered lives. Let us have a sampling or two of Chaucer's illimitable style (albeit in a watered-down modern rendition as the poet's original Middle English style may prove virtually incomprehensible to the modern reader).

> Greyhounds he [the monk] had, as swift as birds, to course
> Hunting a hare or riding at a fence
> Was all his fun, he spared for no expense (Prologue, ll. 194-196).

Brother Hubert, a mendicant friar, was a notorious lecher. He deceived innocent and simple-minded country folk claiming to possess a special license from the pope to hear confession and pronounce absolution, all for a gift, of course! Yet another pilgrim was a pardoner with a wallet brimful of pardons, come all hot from Rome, to sell to the highest bidders! He made a fortune selling fake relics to unsuspecting pious folk.

> In his trunk he had a pillow-case
> Which he asserted was Our Lady's veil.
> He said he had a gobbet of the sail
> Saint Peter had the time when he made bold
> To walk the waves, till Jesu Christ took hold (Prologue, ll. 715-719).

His companion the summoner was equally mired in depravity. Chaucer is scathing in his attack on all the ecclesiastics who make their appearance in his poem. However, his engaging humour and mild irony somewhat tones down its severity.

As a matter of fact, the only church official to escape the poet's censure is a country parson. Many believe that the following lines are a portrait of John Wycliffe with whom the poet was personally acquainted.

> A holy-minded man of good renown
> There was, and poor, the Parson to a town,
> Yet he was rich in holy thought and work.
> He also was a learned man, a clerk,
> Who truly knew Christ's gospel and would preach it
> Devoutly to parishioners, and teach it.
> He much disliked extorting tithe or fee,
> Nay rather he preferred beyond a doubt
> Giving to poor parishioners round about
> From his own goods and Easter offering (Prologue, ll. 487-499).

By the time Luther appeared on the scene in the early sixteenth century the Catholic Church had sunk deep into a morass of immorality and had become a cesspool of venality and corruption. It might well be an illuminating experience to cast a backward glance at the process by which by slow degrees the Church had fallen into its dismal state. With the decline and fall of the Roman Empire early in the fifth century and by and large the assumption of its influence and power by the Church, by slow degrees the administrative apparatus of the empire had been taken over by the Church. In this context, one is reminded of an interesting observation made by Bertrand Russell that three streams have flowed into the Catholic Church and commingled their waters in it. Its sacred history and morals are derived from Judaism; its philosophy it borrowed from the Greeks; its administrative machinery it inherited from the Roman Empire.[3] The administrative apparatus of the Catholic Church owed much to the governing structure of the Roman Empire. For example, in the Roman Empire the term 'Curia' which was used to refer to its senate or the senate house today in the Roman Catholic Church designates the papal court, including all its authorities and functionaries. So also 'ecclesia' which means church

---

[3] Bertrand Russell, *A History of Western Philosophy* (New York: Simon and Schuster, 1945), p.301.

originally designated a meeting of the citizens of Rome. Pontiff, which today is used as an appellation for the pope, in the pagan pre-Christian Roman world referred to the high priest. Besides the title of imperator (commander-in-chief), many Roman emperors called themselves pontiffs or high priests. It is superfluous to multiply instances. The fact of the matter is that Christianity had brought with it many novel notions, ideas and concepts for which a new lexis had to be fashioned. The Church adopted the practical expedient of utilising the existing vocabulary but vastly expanding its scope and subtly altering its nuances so that in due course the terms gained an altogether Christian signification. There is no doubt that the administrative apparatus of the Catholic Church owed much to that of imperial Rome.

The pope presided over a bureaucracy and an administration that was systematically organised, yet at the same time was rigidly hierarchical. Next only to the pope and yet at the top of the papal pyramid sat the papal court called the Curia which had in its oversight several departments. The *Rota Romana* or Consistory functioned as the Church's Supreme Court. The Chancery (*Cancellaria Apostolica*) prepared papal documents and bulls. Excommunications, indulgences and similar functions were served by *Poenitentiara Apostolica*. The papal finances were looked after by the Chamber (*Camera Apostolica*). One can very well imagine the scale of expenses involved in the smooth running of this elaborate administrative machine. A highly complex and ingenious system of taxation had been created to meet the ever-growing needs of the Curia. Here are a few of the payments that Rome levied from its constituents. All members of the clergy were required to pay a tenth of their income, officially called tithes, into the papal treasury. A tax called census[4] was levied from rulers

---

[4] Interestingly census comes from the Latin *censere* which means to assess [tax]. We would do well to remember that the purpose of the census ordered by Augustus Caesar at the time of the birth of Jesus was for the assessment of tax.

owing allegiance to the pope as his vassals and from heads of monasteries and other religious foundations under the direct supervision of the pope. Income from vacant benefices also was the prerogative of the pope. Before confirmation in the office, heavy payment for the purchase of the pallium[5] had to be paid by each and every bishop. The higher clergy such as bishops, archbishops and cardinals had to remit their first year's takings — *annates* — to the pope. In *An Appeal to the Ruling Class* Luther explained how the levy came to be arbitrarily enforced. In the context of the peril to Christendom from the Turks the German emperors granted the pope the right to collect annates of all the benefices in Germany to ward off the menace of the enemy. Now, even after the peril had receded, the collection was being continued as though the right had been granted in perpetuity!

In that same publication Luther contended that it was scandalous that a follower of Jesus Christ and a man claiming to be a spiritual descendant of Peter and wearing the Fisherman's Ring lived in such magnificence. The question was of immense topical interest and relevance as under the then reigning Medici pope, Leo X, the papacy had attained the height of extravagance, luxury, ostentation, pomp, splendour and, indeed, sad to say, corruption! The pontiff is reported to have had no fewer than three thousand secretaries alone! His annual income is estimated by Luther to have been an astronomical "ten hundred thousand ducats, not counting the income from the papal estates." When the pope rode out even for entertainment he was accompanied by a retinue of several thousands, even surpassing the progress of kings and emperors in pomp and circumstance. Luther thought that the number of those constituting the pope's retinue and diverse hangers-on ought to be drastically diminished. He was of the strong view that the papacy

---

[5] Pallium is a short woollen cape for which Rome levied a hefty fee. This emblem of a bishop's office and authority could be purchased only from the papal office.

ought to be stripped of its worldly power and material goods to make it more conformable to be a true successor to Peter.

As a matter of fact, we have an exhaustive inventory of papal misdeeds and corrupt financial dealings in the forementioned book. The luxury in which the cardinals lived had stripped monasteries and bishoprics in Italy and Germany of their revenues to such a degree that they had abandoned their Christian service to the people. In many a parish services were no longer held and sermons had ceased to be preached. To reduce the financial burden imposed on parishes, Luther suggests a drastic reduction in the number of serving cardinals. At the time of writing *An Appeal* Luther adduces the scandalous instance of an ecclesiastic who through bribery and corruption had managed to be in possession of twenty-two parishes, seven priories and forty-four canonries and all the revenue that accrued from them! It is superfluous to multiply instances. Suffice it to say that Luther found the Roman See a veritable Aegean stables that badly needed cleansing. "You can find there a buying and selling, a bartering and a bargaining, a lying and trickery, robbery and stealing, pomp, procuration, knavery, and all sorts of stratagems bringing God into contempt, till it would be impossible for the Antichrist to govern more wickedly" (Luther, *An Appeal to the Ruling Class of German Nationality*, Dillenberger, p.429)[6]. Steeped in such gross lethargy and abominable corruption it was too much to expect that the Church would set its house in order. Therefore while the Catholic Church lay stewing in corruption, Luther felt, it was incumbent on the civil authorities to undertake the task of cleansing it of the taint of mismanagement and corrupt practices. In *An Appeal* he made a series of sweeping proposals

---

[6] All quotations from Luther cited as *Dillenberger* are from *Martin Luther: Selections from his Writings*. Ed. John Dillenberger. Anchor Books, Garden City, New York, 1961.

to the emperor and the German princes to arrest the avarice of Rome and restore their own authority and independence.

The Epistle to the Hebrews gives a long list of heroes of faith from the Bible. Few, if any, of the Renaissance popes would qualify for placement in it. By and large, they probably deserve all the opprobrium that has been rained upon them for the decadence and corruption within the corpus of the Catholic Church. Yet, is it not in the interests of justice and fair play that we put the record right by listing their outstanding achievements as lovers of art and beauty and as patrons of artists, if not in the field of spirituality? Thommaso Parentucelli (1398-1455), later Pope Nicholas V (1447-1455), conceived a vision of Renaissance Rome excelling in beauty and grandeur the pagan metropolis of Roman imperialism and laid the early architectural plans for the Eternal City. The well-known art historian Kenneth Clark showers a lavish encomium on men like Nicholas when he characterises the Rome of the Renaissance popes as "the most grandiose piece of town planning ever attempted."[7] Pope Nicholas was an outstanding patron of the arts and humanist scholars such as Leone Battista Alberti (1404-1472). Aeneas Silvius (1405-1464), later Pope Pius II (1458-1464), was a distinguished humanist scholar and man of letters. Hailing from the prominent Italian family of Della Rovere, Francesco della Rovere (1414-1484), later became Pope Sixtus IV. He founded the Vatican Library and made the great humanist scholar Bartolommeo Platina its first prefect. The Sistine Chapel is named after him. His nephew Giuliano della Rovere became Pope Julius II (1503-1513). Julius founded the Vatican Museum and got Michelangelo to paint the ceiling of the Sistine Chapel. He also got Raphael to paint the papal apartments. It was he who conceived the audacious plan to pull down the old St. Peter's, one of the most ancient and venerable churches in Christendom, and build something vastly grander in its

---

[7] Kenneth Clark, *Civilization*, (New York, Harper & Row, 1969), p. 167.

place. Brabanto supplied the plan for it. Although St. Peter's took another century for completion, Julius' ambition gives us a measure of the man. Do these mammoth achievements of the Renaissance popes extenuate their failure as spiritual leaders of the Catholic Church? Hardly, one would think. Nevertheless it is in the fitness of things that we record their achievements as lovers of beauty and art and as outstanding patrons of men of letters and artists.

In the course of our pursuit of Luther's trumpet call for the reform of the Catholic Church, a rather exclusive concentration on the ills besetting it has been a foregone conclusion. However, this is liable to give a rather lop-sided view of the spiritual well-being of Christendom. Even in the purely spiritual realm, the Church had outstanding personalities of sanctity, who by their exemplary holy life would to some degree make amends for the sins of omission and commission of popes, priests, and prelates. To put the record straight it needs to be emphasised that while the rest of Europe languished in the lap of the darkness of ignorance, it was the institutions of the Church such as the monastic orders that kept the light of learning burning brightly. While the Church like a magnet drew towards it some of the most intellectually gifted men like Augustine of Hippo and Thomas Aquinas, equally it was only within its largely democratic ethos that a gifted man from a humble background could rise to great eminence like Thomas, Cardinal Wolsey, a butcher's son who became Archbishop of York and later Lord Chancellor. The rot may have been gnawing into the vitals of the Vatican, but true Christian charity and piety continued to be practised unabated by countless ordinary Christians. Nor were all those connected with religious officialdom idle, avaricious and venal. Numerous humble and devout evangelical workers like Chaucer's poor parson rendered yeoman service as true followers of Jesus. While these must remain anonymous heroes known only to God, there are outstanding leaders possessed of extraordinary religious genius who shine like stars in the annals of the

THE BACKGROUND OF THE REFORMATION 31

Church. A peep into the lives of a few of these towering personalities will help us to come to a balanced view of the state of Christianity in the middle Ages.

The following miniature vignettes of three saintly heroes should by their holy lives serve as lodestars to sinful humanity. If we are asked to pick from the annals of Christianity an individual the pattern of whose life exemplified and imitated that of Jesus, the name of Francis of Assisi would spring up in the minds of most of us. Similarly, if one were asked to name a book of Christian devotional literature, *The Imitation of Christ* by Thomas Kempis would be one's spontaneous choice. So also the Jesuits by their ubiquitous presence in the realm of Christian service, especially in the field of education, call for commendation. Therefore my third choice is Ignatius Loyola, the founder of the Society of Jesus.

The life of Francis of Assisi reads like a fable. In the Italian town of Assisi there lived a rich young dandy by name Francesco[8] (Francis) Bernardone, the son of a wealthy merchant of the town. A great admirer of troubadour poetry and a voracious reader of romances dealing with love and adventure, Francesco led the life of a fashionable young dandy of the time. One fine morning he had fitted himself out in elegant attire and was about to set off on some pleasant jaunt when he met a poor man, and deeply touched by his sad condition, gave away his cloak to him. Thereafter he started giving away all his possessions so much so that, alarmed at his largesse, his father disinherited him. One day during Mass he heard the instructions that Jesus gave to his Apostles as He sent them out on a preaching mission: "Provide neither gold, nor silver, nor brass in your purses. Nor scrip for your journey, neither two coats, neither shoes, nor yet staves: for the workman is worthy of his meat"

---

[8] Francesco in Italian means French. Francesco's father was a frequent visitor to France, especially Paris, on business.

(Matthew 10: 9-10). Profoundly inspired by the message and interpreting it as a call from God, Francis then and there resolved to give up everything. Living in abject poverty, but still nostalgically haunted by the youthful ideals of chivalry, courtesy and honour cherished by him, he said he had taken poverty for his Lady. Soon with a few companions who had gathered around him, the group roamed all over Italy preaching the Gospel and working with their hands to earn their bread. The order of the Franciscans was founded in 1210 in Assisi. Thus began the uncommon fraternity of Franciscan mendicant friars. The older monastic orders had withdrawn to solitary places "far from the madding crowd's ignoble strife." The Franciscans, on the other hand, chose to work in heavily populated cities. Endowed with a poetic temperament and imbued with love for all God's creation, Francis' love was not limited to his fellow human beings, but extended to all living organisms and even to inanimate things.[9] To him fire was not simply one of the elements but brother fire; he called the wind his sister. His "Canticle of the Sun" proclaims his sense of the unity of all creation. His life was distinguished by its intense joyousness despite poverty and self-denial. Worn out by the privations he endured, Francis died in 1226 at the comparatively young age of forty-three. A century later legends and anecdotes about him were collected in the Italian *Fioretti de San Francesco* (*The Little Flowers of St. Francis*). Francis, this supreme religious genius, had indeed attained in his remarkable life "A condition of complete simplicity/ Costing not less than everything."[10] Francis himself was no intellectual and was disdainful of the cold intellectualism of the scholastic philosophers and their hair-splitting dialectics and, in fact, for the academic world on the whole. Francis may have been somewhat of an anti-intellectual, but some of his

---

[9] There is a famous master painting of Francis feeding the birds by the great pre-Renaissance Italian painter Giotto (pronounced 'joto').

[10] T. S. Eliot, "Little Gidding," ll. 255-256.

followers established themselves early in the emerging universities of Paris, Oxford and Cambridge. Among the great philosophers, dialecticians, scholars and teachers of their time were Roger Bacon, Duns Scotus and William of Ockham, all Franciscans.

Our second example, Thomas á Kempis, the compiler of the wonderful little primer on spiritual life called the *Imitation of Christ* (*Imitatio Christi*) illustrates an important facet of medieval Christianity, namely, the life of contemplation. He was born at Kempen near Dusseldorf in 1380. As a very young man he joined the Congregation of the Common Life, a community wedded to the practice of Christian life as it was lived in apostolic times. The *Imitation* glows with Thomas's love of God. Its theme is God's love, mercy and holiness. With his profound knowledge of the Scriptures, his deep humility and his understanding of the spiritual needs of man, Thomas is an unerring guide to all who long to live a life filled with the love, peace and joy that Jesus brought into the world. The *Imitation* has influenced the life of millions all over the world for centuries and brought solace to all who seek to find peace and happiness in life.

If the life of the author of the *Imitation* illustrates the contemplative aspect of Christian living, Ignatius Loyola's (1491-1556) career illuminates its active counterpart. The scion of the Spanish ducal house of Loyola, he was a soldier by profession, but was compelled to leave the army on being severely wounded at the siege of Pamplona in 1521. A fervent devotee of the Virgin Mary, he is the founder of the Society of Jesus, the Jesuit Order. The Jesuits, principally active in the field of education, render outstanding service to humanity in many parts of the world. *The Spiritual Exercises* (1548) of Ignatius Loyola is a manual of devotions and prayers conducive to religious contemplation leading to mystical vision. These examples of illustrious followers of the life and example of Jesus reveal that, while all may not have been well with the Church establishment, the Good News and the love, peace and joy that Jesus brought into the world were being widely disseminated by His devout followers.

In the eyes of historians almost every epoch in the story of man is a transitional period, generally transiting from a more rudimentary to a better, more advanced state. It is in this sense that, significantly, Jacob Bronowski calls his story of the development of human culture and science, *The Ascent of Man*.[11] But there are just a very few times in history when man made a sudden and extraordinary leap forward and the times we are now concerned with — the period of the Reformation — was certainly one such. Due to the congruence of a variety of dynamic forces, throughout Western Europe there was this extraordinary outpouring of energy, an intensification of life forces. Therefore there is special justification for regarding sixteenth-century Europe as a watershed in human history. Like any other development in human culture, it is a just and legitimate exercise to look at the Reformation from a limited, acute angle as a purely religious ferment. But in order to appreciate its true impact and to see it in its proper perspective, it is best to look at it as but one aspect, be it a very important aspect, of a myriad-faceted transformation taking place almost simultaneously all over Europe in several other areas of human endeavour. The numerous geographical explorations, the invention of printing, the Renaissance, and the Reformation, were all part of man's relentless quest for freedom, freedom of thought, of expression, of movement. The combined dynamics of these developments resulted in a gigantic release of liberating, creative and life-enhancing human energies that has enabled us to leave the dark ages far behind us and has given us a fresh fillip to our forward march into modern history. Owing to the cumulative

---

[11] Jacob Bronowski, *The Ascent of Man* (Boston: Little, Brown, 1973). Originally presented as a thirteen-episode television series by the B.B.C., it was later published as a book.

operation of these momentous events and innovations, in retrospect, mid-sixteenth-century Europe will be seen as a turning point in human history.

The single event that triggered the search for a sea route to the East was the capture of Constantinople by the Ottoman Turks in 1453. This effectively barred Europe from the lucrative trade in luxury goods, silks and spices that the fastidious palates and tastes of the royal courts, the nobility, the merchant princes and the rising middle classes had got accustomed to. However, the ever-expanding horizon that the geographical adventurers opened out to us resulted in not merely an enlargement of our notions regarding the shape and expanse of our space, but equally an enlargement of our minds and sensibilities too. The mariners who sailed forth into hitherto unknown and unexplored seas and lands, men like Cabot, Magellan, Raleigh, Drake, and the like, may have been no nobler, in the strict sense, than pirates and buccaneers. Their patrons, the rulers of Portugal, Spain and England may have been motivated by no nobler sentiments than the base lure of gold. But the outcome was an overall enrichment and expansion of our physical and mental horizons by our exposure to new cultures, peoples and products. Indeed, with the opening up of the new sea-routes to Asia, the West Indies and the Americas, the Mediterranean gradually lost its prominence as the hub of maritime commerce until the opening of the Suez Canal in 1869 when it regained its utility as one of the most important waterways of the world.

The pan-European intellectual and cultural awakening known as the Renaissance opened up our mental horizons like no other development in human evolution. The impact of the New Learning on European culture was profound and transformational. During the depredations that accompanied the rapid rise and expansion of Islam as a political power and in the new faith's over-weening zeal for iconoclasm, much of mankind's heritage in the form of precious manuscripts, art objects, etc., were ruthlessly vandalized and thus irretrievably lost to posterity. However, there was a silver lining in this otherwise sorry saga. While Europe slept in ignorance of its classical heritage, some Arab scholars preserved the classics of Greek philosophy, mathematics and medicine in Arabic translations. It was the re-discovery by Europe of these long-lost classics of Greece and Rome, their art, architecture and sculpture that gave birth to the Renaissance. The urbane, humane values that the re-discovered Greek and Roman classics opened out to our amazing eyes greatly expanded human sensibility. The spirit of rational inquiry and discourse that the study of the classics engendered helped in fostering a scientific temper in society and accounted for the rapid progress of science in the coming years.

It is futile on our part to try to truly gauge the importance to the march of civilization of the invention of printing.[12] It was surely as transformative to fifteenth-century Europe as the internet revolution has been to ours. With the ease and rapidity with which the accumulated wit and wisdom of the human race could be multiplied and disseminated, we have truly emerged from the crippling darkness of ignorance into the marvellous light of knowledge. It may not be inappropriate here to add something further on the new trade of printing and the new class of entrepreneurs called printers. The first book to be printed from movable types is believed to have been the Gutenberg Bible. It is also known as the Mazarin Bible because it was discovered in the library of Cardinal Mazarin in Paris in 1760. It was an edition of the Latin Vulgate printed in 1455 at Mainz, Germany using Gothic types. Interestingly, for a

---

[12] Printing from movable type was invented by Johann Gutenberg, a goldsmith from Mainz, Germany, in 1456. Improving upon the then available technologies, and by devising a mould for casting a regularly-sized and spaced metal types, an ink that would adhere to the type and a press that can leave a lasting impression on paper, he succeeded in turning out products of superior quality in layout and typography from the very beginning.

THE BACKGROUND OF THE REFORMATION 37

fairly long time after the introduction of printing, the specimens of the art and craft of the printer that have come down to us hardly resemble the printed volumes that we are all familiar with today. As their models were the beautifully wrought illuminated manuscript books, naturally, the early printed books looked rather like replicas of the handwritten copies. Moreover, the early editions used a large format and were quite expensive. Some, like Bibles, were printed on vellum using gold and silver lettering and had illuminations, like manuscripts. Many of the early printed books can well and truly be called *objets d'art*. Owing to the several special characteristics shared by books produced during the early period of printing, especially before 1500, they are called incunabula. The Vatican libraries are a treasure-house of incunabula. England was rather late in adopting the new technology. It is estimated that eight European countries took precedence of England in this respect. Interestingly it was Germans who set up printing presses in many of the European countries. Printing was brought to England from Flanders by William Caxton, who set up a printing press in Westminster, London, in 1476. One of the early volumes to be issued by Caxton's press was *The Canterbury Tales* by Geoffrey Chaucer.

The coming together of the temper of ratiocination fostered by the men of the New Learning and the power of the printing press was a truly explosive mixture. Let me illustrate the truth of this assertion using just a single example. One of the foremost exponents of classical studies at this time in Europe was Erasmus of Rotterdam. His edition of the Greek New Testament, the first-ever New Testament in its original Greek to be released in print, was a historic event. Strongly reminiscent of manuscript books, it was a beautiful volume, the text accompanied by illuminating annotations as well as a Latin translation. Soon after its publication in 1516, Luther received his copy. It was from Erasmus' explanatory notes that Luther understood the correct sense of Jesus' exhortation to repent. Erasmus' annotation clarified that Jesus' exhortation to repent did not mean 'do penance' as the Catholic Church interpreted it, but that it really was a call to be penitent. The effect of Erasmus' Bible on the path the Reformation was to adopt was considerable. The glosses that Erasmus appended in his edition to key words like ecclesia, bishop and the like and the subtle nuances to these concepts introduced by the glosses played a not insignificant role in influencing the tempo of the Reformation Movement. Besides this, several subsequent renderings of the New Testament into European languages were made from Erasmus' edition. Erasmus made two lifelong friends: one Sir Thomas More of England—of whom more will be said when we discuss the English Reformation—and the second one the great Protestant and humanist printer Johann Froben (Frobenius in Latin) of Basel, Switzerland. It was from Froben's press that Erasmus' Greek New Testament saw the light of day. The books, most of them classics, printed by Frobenius were objects of rare beauty and outstanding examples of the art of the printer. It is extremely doubtful whether the new notions of the reformers would have spread like wild fire had it not been for the almost magical power of the printing press!

The wind of change was blowing all across Europe. Yet the Catholic Church, impervious to all change, went on in its accustomed fashion till it was rudely awakened by Luther's call to reform.

Chapter 4

THE LIFE OF MARTIN LUTHER

> (O Deutschland, double a desperate name!
> O world wide of its good!
> But Gertrude, lily, and Luther, are two of a town,
> Christ's lily and beast of the waste wood:
> From life's dawn it is drawn down,
> Abel is Cain's brother and breasts they have sucked the same.)[1]

The foregoing uncharitable and venomous phillipic against Luther by the Jesuit-turned-poet Hopkins is probably an extreme and abnormal response to the reform movement initiated and launched by him. However, one cannot help but exclaim in disbelief whether religious vitriol can wound any sharper or sectarian bigotry rise any higher. Nevertheless, however atypical, it should give one some notion of the reaction that it still evokes in the hearts and minds of many Christians. However, irrational prejudice and resulting hostility are not confined to any one of the Christian sects. For example, there are not a few who think that the great Puritan poet Milton's depiction of the enthroned Satan in Pandemonium is a derisive description of the papal throne.

---

[1] Gerard Manley Hopkins, "The Wreck of the Deutschland," Lines 155-160. Musing on the fact that St. Gertrude (a thirteenth-century Christian saint [c. 1256-c. 1302] who lived in a convent near Eisleben in Saxony) and Martin Luther hailed from the same German town of Eisleben, the poet compares them to Abel and Cain respectively who emerged from the same womb, one a righteous man and the other a fratricide. Abel and Cain were sons of Adam and Eve. On the sacrifice of Abel of the firstlings of his flock proving more acceptable to God, out of jealousy Cain killed his brother. The analogy may be grossly inappropriate and vicious. Be that as it may, Hopkins' point seems to be that Luther's action in ripping apart the holy, apostolic Catholic Church is like Cain shedding his brother's blood.

> High on a throne of royal state, which far
> Outshone the wealth of Ormus and of Ind,
> Or where the gorgeous East with richest hand
> Showers on her kings barbaric pearl and gold,
> Satan exalted sat....[2]

Nevertheless, it is important to keep clear of all extreme views and look at people, places and events with a dispassionate eye. In order to assist the reader to arrive at a sane, mature and sober perspective on Luther the man and his mammoth achievements, let us juxtapose Hopkins' extreme and sensational view with a polar opposite prospect of the reformer. In 1837-40, the nineteenth-century English writer Thomas Carlyle (1795-1881) — Carlyle was in fact a Scotsman — delivered a series of lectures in London setting out his philosophy of history. These were later published under the title *On Heroes, Hero-Worship and the Heroic in History*. Carlyle believed that history is the record of the thoughts and actions of great men. He believed that it is the personality of great men which gives human history its dynamic and momentum. As defined by him, greatness lies in the exercise of heroic virtues, as for example, in the will to renounce or the power to achieve. For his heroes Carlyle chose typical and outstanding examples of men who demonstrated uncommon excellence in different arenas of human endeavour. For the hero as poet he picked Dante and Shakespeare, unexcelled in world literature for the sweep of their imagination and their generous humanity. Samuel Johnson, Jean Jacques Rousseau and Robert Burns were his choice for hero as man of letters. For the hero as king he selected Cromwell and Napoleon. What is significant for us to note here is that for hero as priest his choice fell on Martin Luther [and John Knox]. The foregoing pair of polarities, violent vitriol on the part of Hopkins on the one hand, and warm admiration on the part of Carlyle on the other, should enable the judicious reader to arrive at a

---

[2] *Paradise Lost*, Book II: ll. 1-5.

balanced, dispassionate attitude to Luther and the Reformation. We might well lament the manner in which the Holy, Catholic[3] and Apostolic Church was rent asunder by the Reformation. Yet the believer can take comfort in the thought that the Church, Corpus Christi, the true Body of Christ, is a mystical and spiritual entity comprising all the faithful and not the mere visible establishment splintered into a multiplicity of denominations and sects that we sadly witness today.

Towards the close of his life—in 1545, a year before he died—bowing to pressure from solicitous well-wishers and friends, Luther brought out a complete edition of his Latin writings. In the Preface to that work he, for the first time, opened his heart to share many vital memories from his early life, especially regarding his spiritual regeneration and the subsequent progression of his inner life. Perhaps, misled by his confession that what he has furnished are but "confused lucubrations [sic]," some carping critics have cast doubts on the accuracy of Luther's old-age recollections. Nevertheless, handled with due diligence, they do provide valuable insights into the making of the future reformer. Therefore we intend to weave the memories, wherever appropriate, into the following chronicle of the central events of Luther's life.

Martin Luther came of peasant stock. Starting life as a miner, Martin's father Hans Luther turned to the copper mining trade and became relatively prosperous. Martin's mother Margarethe Ziegler belonged to a family of a slightly superior social standing. When Martin came into the world on 10 November 1483 in Eisleben, Thurangia,[4] owing to the

---

[3] The true meaning of 'Catholic' is 'universal'. "Catholic: In ecclesiastical use,1. Of or belonging to the church universal; 2. Of or belonging to the church universal as organized on an accepted basis of faith and order; of the true apostolic Church, orthodox; 3. As applied (since the Reformation) to the Church of Rome= Roman Catholic" (SOED).

[4] Interestingly, the great German musical composer and distinguished organist Johann Sebastian Bach (1685-1750), who later set many of Luther's

precarious state of the infant's health, it was baptized the very next day. In the summer of 1484 the family moved to Mansfeld, another neighbouring town, also in Thurangia. Starting his schooling at the Latin School in Mansfeld, in 1497 he moved to the school run by the Brethren of the Common Life (a Brotherhood resembling an Order)[5] in Magdeburg. Next year he joined St. George's Parish School in Eisenach. In May 1501 he enrolled at Erfurt University to do a basic course in the Liberal Arts. He secured a bachelor's degree in 1502 and was awarded a Master of Arts (*Magister Artium*) degree in January 1505. It may need emphasis here that the language of instruction at the time, as indeed for the next few centuries, all over Europe, was Latin. For the past several centuries what ensured certain success in life in Catholic Christendom had been—and continued to be for the next couple of centuries too—a mastery of the Latin tongue because proficiency in this learned language was the royal road to success in life as it was the language of the Church, of the law courts, both civil and ecclesiastical, of diplomacy, of the learned professions, of trade and travel. Martin emerged from his school and university career as an accomplished scholar in this indispensable medium for advancement in life. Hans, the elder Luther, wanted his son to pursue canon law, a respectable and lucrative profession, and so, bowing to his father's wishes, Martin enrolled himself as a student in the Faculty of Law at Erfurt University. Yet, despite his father's plan and his own compliance to it, events, as they turned out, took a very different and unexpected turn. Soon after joining the legal faculty, on 2 July, on his way home, near Erfurt, he was struck by a violent bolt of lightning and felled to the ground. Almost involuntarily,

---

hymns to music was also born in Eisleben. Thurangia was a state in Central Germany. It is good to keep in mind the fact that the political map of Medieval Europe differed substantially from what it is today. Germany, as we know it today (or Italy, for that matter), is a much later formation.

[5] Thomas á Kempis, the celebrated author of *Imitation of Christ* had been a member of this order.

the ejaculatory prayer 'St. Anne,[6] help, I will become a monk' escaped his lips. True to his vow, two weeks later Martin Luther presented himself at the Black Monastery of the Augustinian Hermits at Erfurt and was enrolled as a novice. On entering the monastery as a novice, Luther received a copy of the Bible bound in red leather, as ordered by his Superior Johannes von Staupitz who had some time earlier instituted Biblical study at his monastery, a rather uncommon innovation at the time at any medieval monastery. Thus began his life-long and passionate engagement with the Sacred Scriptures.

Even though he had irrevocably committed himself to leading a monastic life as a member of the Augustinian Order, when he took the final monastic vows in the autumn of 1506, Luther found himself more and more continuously assailed by spiritual doubts and tormented by religious conflicts and inner turmoil. Despite his systematic observance of all the remedies prescribed by the Church, namely, confessions, penance, fasts, whippings, and vigils, his mental turbulence and spiritual disquiet received little respite. Irrespective of the disquiet within, his life as a monk followed its routine progression. Having been ordained a priest in April 1507, he celebrated his first Mass on 2nd May. Providentially at this critical time in his spiritual life he discovered a real mentor in Abbot Staupitz who exerted a benign and paternal influence on him. Instigated and inspired by his superior, Luther began to study theology. He became a bachelor of theology in March 1509 and a doctor of theology in 1512.

During the period 1510-11 he was one of a two-member delegation deputed to Rome to represent certain matters pertaining to their Order before the Roman Curia. Luther would have been woefully obtuse and myopic if he were not appalled by the scale of corruption and moral decrepitude

---

[6] St. Anne is the patron saint of miners.

that he witnessed there in every organ of the Church. Be that as it may, as a pious Catholic, his real feelings were perhaps ambivalent; wonder and amazement at the splendour and majesty of the Church's edifices and monuments and sadness and dejection at its spiritual and moral degeneracy. On his return he was sent to Wittenberg as sub-prior to the monastery there. From the foregoing account of the education and training that Luther had thus far received, it becomes evident that he was the product of a typically medieval religious instruction. There was nothing in it whatsoever that presaged the future revolutionary and reformer. Looking back to those early days, Luther later described himself as a "most enthusiastic papist, submerged in the pope's dogmas."

In 1502, at the invitation of Frederick the Wise, Elector[7] of Saxony, Staupitz established a university in Wittenberg.[8] There he instituted a new professorship of the Bible, a rather uncommon distinction for any medieval university, with himself filling the chair till 1512, at which time Luther was called upon to assume the position. It should be emphasized at this point that although he was a doctor of theology he had not seriously studied the Bible so far, the reason being that the study of the Bible was given scant attention within the theology curriculum at a medieval university. Now that his position required him to lecture on the Bible and explicate its various books, Luther perforce sought a serious engagement with the Bible. This marked a real turning point in his life. As professor of theology the first series of lectures that he delivered was on Genesis. In hindsight the year 1513 can be seen as a period of spiritual crisis in Luther's life. In the spring of that year he had a remarkable mystical revelation in the Tower of the Black Monastery. While he was pondering upon and wrestling with Paul's Epistle to the

---

[7] Electors were German princes entitled to elect the Holy Roman Emperor.

[8] Shakespeare's hero Prince Hamlet is portrayed as a pupil in Wittenberg University.

Romans he encountered an acute knot at Romans 1:17: 'the righteousness of God'. He had been intellectually and spiritually confused because the scholastics such as Duns Scotus, Peter Lombard and Thomas Aquinas had expounded *iustus dues* [God's justice] as the aspect of God that avenges and punishes the sinner for his transgression of God's law. But that was to miss the heart of the Gospel which proclaims God's own solution to the dilemma by sending His own Son in the likeness of sinful man. By virtue of Christ's personal act of atonement, through faith we are now able to reach reconciliation with the just God and achieve salvation. In other words Christ's vicarious sacrifice has now rendered salvation a matter of belief in Christ rather than something to be achieved through meritorious works. The key that unlocked the mystery for Luther was Romans 1:17: "For the Good News reveals God's way of putting people right with Himself—it is by faith from beginning to end. As the Scripture says, 'Those made right with God by faith will live'" (The New Translation). It was the shock of the illuminating revelation on reading that verse that led to Luther's liberating and exhilarating experience of conversion and assurance of salvation. During his almost mystical experience in the Tower, as in an epiphany, Luther at last saw the light. Christ, having achieved our righteousness through His sacrificial death on the cross, bestows it freely upon all believers. Luther felt as though this single verse had illumined the path of salvation and swung open the gates of paradise to him. Did the revelation in the Tower plant the seeds of the Reformation in Luther's mind, one is left to ponder.

If the sinner is justified by faith alone and not by what he has done or not done, and if salvation depends upon the simple response of the believing heart to Jesus Christ and the Word of God, we arrive at its logical conclusion that the whole system of sacerdotalism is rendered redundant and even ineffective. Obviously this Reformation faith cut at the root of the Catholic Church's emphasis on priestly ministration and intercession in the dispensation of the sacraments and all other indispensable ecclesiastical rites and ceremonies which too are essential concomitants to salvation besides faith. And what is the role of works such as penance, pilgrimage, fasting, and all other associated rites and observances? They too are rendered null and void of all utility. From this vantage point namely that faith alone counts for salvation, it is easy to see how Luther came to believe in the priesthood of all the faithful people of God. This hugely liberating awareness on the part of Luther can be seen in hindsight as the cornerstone of his disagreements with the Catholic Church. In his firm conviction that it is the free grace of God that sets the sinner right in the sight of God we have the Reformation principles in their germinal state. Although it took the indulgence controversy and protracted tussle with the Roman Church for the full flowering of the Reformation, it is not difficult to visualize it as a natural development, almost a foregone conclusion, from this fundamental faith of the Christian.

The Indulgence Controversy

In the three or four years that elapsed following his climacteric spiritual vision, Luther pored over the Bible and brought forth his penetrating series of lectures on the Psalms, Romans and Galatians. His intense and continual close encounter with the Word of God enabled him to see it in a fresh and illuminating flash of insight. In the light of this new revelation, he became sceptical and highly critical of the role of sacraments in a Christian's personal redemption. Moreover, he saw the futility of many of the rituals, ceremonies and practices within the Church as of little avail in attaining one's spiritual destination. Salvation being God's gratuitous gift, Luther was assailed by doubts as to whether the Church's teaching regarding the accumulation of merit through sacraments, pilgrimages, relics, indulgences, indeed the whole host of religious rigmarole of rituals and ceremonies, was not one grand folly. He was justly revolted by the sad spectacle of the several echelons of the ecclesiastical hierarchy so steeped in venality and cupidity as to make merchandise of the Church's sacraments, benefices and even salvation itself.

While indulgence preachers- called *quaestors*[9] —went all over the country exhorting the people to buy pardon for their sins for cash payment to the Church, Luther tried to dissuade them from this fraudulent and futile practice. We can clearly perceive that his attitude and the stand he took had full Biblical authority behind them. When we turn to Scripture we find in Peter's words to Simon, the sorcerer: "You cannot buy the gift of God with money" a clear endorsement of Luther's stand. How presumptuous of one, whether one is a priest or a layman, to imagine that forgiveness for sins of commission or omission can be purchased with money?

Even at the risk of taking the reader on a rather lengthy digression, it seems incumbent on my part to furnish adequate background information on the whole controversy surrounding the sale of indulgences. Indulgences pertain to the highly complex and involved sacrament of penance developed by the medieval Catholic Church. It has its origin in Christ's call to the people who flocked to hear His Good News to repent and be ready to enter the Kingdom of God (Matthew 4:17; Mark 1:15). The sermons of Peter and Paul emphasized repentance of sins and belief in Jesus the Messiah as pre-requisites for salvation. Unfortunately the Greek verb for 'to repent' gave rise to two interpretations: a) to repent and b) to do penance. Thomas Aquinas, with his genius for systematizing and codifying every branch of knowledge known at that time, worked out an elaborate theology of penitential acts. Penance comprised four elements: contrition,

---

[9] Originally, in the Roman Empire, a *quaestor* was an official in charge of public funds.

confession, satisfaction and absolution and the sinner must, with the Church's guidance through the first three steps secure his absolution and that too through the Church's ministration. The medieval Church taught that one way of doing it was to go in for the purchase of an indulgence. Thus started the grand folly of simple, credulous folk deluded into believing that a papal indulgence absolved them of part or all of their sins for a certain amount of money paid into the Church's coffers.

The Roman Church's elaborate instruction regarding penance led to yet another doctrine not really found in the New Testament. Closely connected with its teaching on the sacrament of penance, gradually there developed in the medieval Church the doctrine of purgatory. It rests on an extremely tenuous and slippery foundation. It is difficult to find any Biblical sanction or warranty for it. The text cited in support of it is Jesus' words: "I tell you the truth, you will not get out until you have paid the last penny" (Matthew 5: 26). The context makes it explicit that the words do not even remotely indicate any suggestion of the purgation of sin. On the contrary, would not Christ's comforting words from the cross to the repentant thief, "To day shalt thou be with me in paradise" seem to obviate the presence of a middle state? Be that as it may, despite all the evidence to the contrary, apologists of purgatory cite patristic warrant for their support of the doctrine. Belief in the concept seems to have originated with the Alexandrian Fathers. Origen (2nd century), for instance, curiously interpreted Matthew 5:26 as an allegory for a state of the soul's catharsis to rid it of any residual sins. We do find a clear statement regarding a middle region in Augustine of Hippo's magnum opus *Civitas Dei contra Gentiles* (*The City of God against the City of the Pagans*). The following extract from Augustine "As for temporal pain, some endure it here and some hereafter, and some both here and there; yet all is past before the Last Judgement" (*City of God*, xxi:13) is a clear adumbration of Purgatory. The proponent of a full-fledged theory of purgatory, a middle state between heaven and hell, however, is Thomas Aquinas.[10]

It is time we got back on the trail of the indulgence controversy. It is instructive to look at, in some detail, the immediate context of Luther's proposition to challenge the sale of indulgences. Time and again the medieval Catholic Church had resorted to trafficking in indulgences to overcome financial exigencies. The indulgences offered were either partial which effected forgiveness for part of one's sins or plenary which wiped off all major sins. Indulgences were first offered for sale to raise funds to fight the First Crusade. Thereafter archbishops, cardinals and popes had, on and off, indulged in the trade sometimes solely with an eye for making a profit. Finally, to prevent misuse, the right to sell indulgences had been reserved to the pope alone. Let us now examine the special circumstances in which Luther's confrontation with the papacy regarding the erroneous custom occurred. It began with Pope Leo X's proclamation in 1515 of a plenary indulgence in order to finance the construction of the new St. Peter's which had been begun by his predecessor Julius II. Meanwhile, the archdiocese of Mainz—the see of the primate of all Germany, the largest in Christendom—fell vacant. The position could be filled only by a candidate willing and able to afford a huge payment—10,000 ducats to be exact—for the pallium and for confirmation in the position. Albrecht, the younger brother of the Elector of Brandenburg, was eager for the position and ready to raise the cash necessary. However, a papal dispensation—which involved an additional payment of 11,000 ducats—was needed as Albrecht was already archbishop of Magdeburg. The banking house of Fuggers, bankers to the Vatican, advanced the needed fund of 21,000

---

[10] Cantica II, *Il Purgatorio* (*Purgatory*) of *The Comedy of Dante Alighieri* (commonly called *The Divine Comedy*) is firmly and closely built on Aquinas' ideas. I am a great admirer of Dante and enjoy his superb poetry and his supreme craftsmanship, though no devotee of the notion of purgatory.

ducats—really an enormous sum of money when you compute its purchasing value at the time—on the understanding that half the money raised by the sale of indulgences within the archbishop's jurisdiction would go to repay the Fuggers' loan, while the other half would flow into the coffers of the Vatican. This is the sordid background of Leo's bull of indulgence titled *Sacrosancti salvatoris et redemptoris nostris* of 31 March 1515

It was in the context of the widespread abuse of the Church's ministry that on 31 October 1517 Luther penned two letters in Latin which, although unbeknown to anyone at the time, were but the prelude to the Reformation movement that drastically changed not only the Catholic Church, but the face of European society as well. The first one against the sale of indulgences[11]—being conducted in the background of Johann Tetzel's sermons on indulgences—was addressed to Archbishop Albrecht of Mainz, who, as has been already mentioned, received half of the proceeds of the sale. That the other half went to enrich the coffers of the Vatican was a fact unknown to Luther at the time, according to his own admission. The second one addressed to Bishop Jerome of Magdeburg enclosed Luther's 95 Theses[12] denouncing the abuse of indulgences and offering his readiness to participate in an academic disputation[13] on the topic with anyone willing to pick up the gauntlet. Both the letters were a cry from the heart of a young, loyal and pious Catholic priest and scholar to put a stop to the sale of the

---

[11] Indulgences: From *indulgentia* (Latin for 'kindness'): "a remission of the punishment which is still due to sin after sacramental absolution, this remission being valid in the court of conscience and before God, and being made by an application of the treasure of the Church on the part of a lawful superior" (SOED).

[12] The original title was "Disputation on the Power and Efficacy of Indulgences." The document comprised ninety-five theses and soon acquired the popular name "The Ninety-five Theses".

[13] Disputation: (specifically) "An exercise in which parties formally sustain, attack, and defend a thesis, as in the medieval universities" (SOED).

grace of God which demanded neither silver nor gold but is freely available to all believers who were ready to confess and turn away from their sinful ways. "But the poor little brother was despised," lamented Luther, writing about it later. (Luther, "Preface to Latin Writings," Dillenberger, p.5). The same day the Theses alone were posted on the door of the Wittenberg *Schlosskirche* (Castle Church).

In the light of the transformation of European society that this seemingly simple and innocuous act culminated in, it is important to emphasize that the posting of the theses was nothing unusual or extraordinary. As a matter of fact disputations were quite a common form of intellectual exercise in those days and formed part and parcel of academic life at a medieval university. The modern reader probably needs to be reminded that disputations and debates were purely academic exercises which generally led to no concrete actions. Unlike many other institutions, the medieval university was largely a democratic institution and much leeway was permitted in academic discussion even in religious matters. Moreover there was nothing really revolutionary in Luther's ideas. Before him several humanists and even men of the cloth had tried to expose the Church's shortcomings. In the Preface cited earlier, Luther clearly states that he "got into these turmoils [sic] by accident and not by will or intention." A longer excerpt from Luther's Preface mentioned earlier seems appropriate to clarify his attitude.

> Hence, when in the year 1517 indulgences were sold (I wanted to say promoted) in these regions for most shameful gain—I was then a preacher, a young doctor of theology, so to speak—and I began to dissuade the people and to urge them not to listen to the clamours of the indulgence hawkers; they had better things to do. I certainly thought that in this case I should have a protector in the pope, on whose trustworthiness I then leaned strongly, for in his decrees he most clearly damned the immoderation of the quaestors, as he called the indulgence preachers" (Luther, "Preface to Latin Writings," Dillenberger, p.5).

A review of the Theses bears out the truth of Luther's statement. Yet it is amazing that Luther was naïve enough to imagine that the pope who was the beneficiary of the sale would vindicate his opposition! It even makes one wonder whether Luther was under some misapprehension that the transaction had not received the pope's mandate. There is even a tacit admission on the part of the prospective disputant that in certain circumstances the pope may indeed grant remission of sins. For example, thesis 38 clearly says "the pope's remission and dispensation are in no way to be despised, for... they proclaim the divine remission." Moreover, apart from the theses, in March 1518 in a publication called *Sermon on Indulgences* and in *The Explanations of the Ninety-five Theses* (August 1518), Luther expressed the view that indulgences should not be condemned but that acts of charity should be preferred to them. Throughout the theses the disputant leaves considerable scope for compromise to accommodate the pope's sensibility. However, while he does not dispute the authority of the pope as head of the Catholic Church, he does express his misgivings regarding his divine rights. So there was much in the theses to annoy Rome. Was Luther blissfully oblivious of the risks and perils he was courting? The preamble to the Disputation is couched in the conventional form prevalent in the medieval university. Here is a young priest and scholar, out of his love and concern for the truth, inviting all interested parties to participate in a rational discourse, either orally or in writing, on a matter of vital public interest. The amplitude of the theses clearly bears out Luther's analytical skills. The objective seems to be to provoke a wide-ranging rational debate by looking at the central thesis from multiple perspectives. However, what the document makes plain is that the focus of the proposed disputation was to deliver a frontal attack on the swift-spreading abuse of indulgence-hawking from a multitude of standpoints. However pure and lofty Luther's intention might have been, the dynamic of history, as we now know, produced quite unintended consequences.

What happened in the present case was that shortly after the posting of the Theses, copies found their way into the hands of numerous scholars and other well-wishers of the author and disputant. Even then, the document had but a limited reach as it was framed in the learned language of Latin. But it did not take long for the Theses to be turned into German and disseminated widely. They soon found an unexpected resonance in many people's thinking, as there had for long existed widespread resentment at Rome's avaricious monetary exactions to maintain the luxurious lifestyle of its bloated bureaucracy and its many religious rituals and services. This popular mood of resentment against the papacy was only further aggravated when Luther explained the basic ideas of the Theses in his vernacular publication "A Sermon on Indulgence and Grace," though, ironically as it seems to us, the author's intended aim as stated in "Preface to Latin Writings" was to mollify the pope's feelings.

Luther's maiden appearance at an academic debate was at the Augustinian Convent in Heidelberg when he stood up to defend his Theses. Meanwhile, on 7 August Rome pronounced the Theses heretical and Pope Leo X[14] summoned the heretic to Rome to stand trial before the papal court within sixty days. Rome's reaction could well have been anticipated; yet Luther appears to have been initially shocked and alarmed when he was, in his own words, "accused by the pope, cited to Rome, and the whole papacy" rose as one body against him. However, the prompt intervention of Frederick the Wise, the Elector of Saxony—the region where Luther lived—in the affair, forestalled the Vatican's inquisition. Alternatively, it was arranged that Luther would be given a hearing in Augsburg by Cardinal Cajetan, the

---

[14] Giovanni de Medici, afterwards Pope Leo X, was the son of Lorenzo de Medici. Poet, patron of the arts and literature, Lorenzo (1449-92), called the Magnificent, was the ruler of the Renaissance city-state of Florence from 1478-92. Leo X was one of several members of the Medici family to adorn the papal throne.

papal legate. Let us listen in to Luther's own account. "So I came to Augsburg, afoot and poor, supplied with food and letters of recommendation from Prince Frederick" (Luther, "Preface to Latin Writings," Dillenberger, p.6). Luther was warned by friends not to take the risk of going to Augsburg to appear before the cardinal without the emperor's safe conduct. So, armed with a safe conduct, Luther presented himself before Cajetan on the third day. This led to no resolution of the conflict as the cardinal's demand that Luther recant his views was summarily rejected by the latter. With the threat of excommunication now looming large, Luther would have been in real peril had it not been for the unstinted support of Frederick which sustained him and saw him through the present crisis as well as several more in the coming days. Meanwhile in February 1519 Emperor Maximilian died and Duke Frederick was elevated to the position of Deputy, thereby strengthening the position of the duke as well as that of his protégé, Luther. Here is Luther's own account of the situation.

> Thereupon the storm ceased to rage a bit, and gradually contempt of excommunication or papal thunderbolts arose. For when Eck brought a bull from Rome condemning Luther . . . Frederick was most indignant. The prince, endowed with incredible insight, caught on to the devices of the Roman Curia and knew how to deal with them in a becoming manner, for he had a keen nose and smelled more and farther than the Romanists could hope or fear (Luther, "Preface to Latin Writings," Dillenberger, p.7).

In the meanwhile as Luther was quick to add, with the Elector's goodwill, the Gospel of Christ was making rapid strides throughout his dominions and consequently the cause of the papacy suffered great damage.

Yet another debate held at the University of Leipzig with John Eck, a professor at the University of Ingolstadt—an out-and-out Roman sympathiser—too failed to effect a reconciliation of the views of the warring parties. What really happened at this forum was that it not only failed to achieve a rapprochement of views, but that on the contrary it further alienated the contending parties. As might well have been predicated, post-Leipzig debate we do discern a further hardening of Luther's stand. This new turn of events was evidenced by the fact that his stated position now went beyond his opposition to the sale of indulgences and called into question the doctrine of the infallibility of popes and councils, and by implication, all man-made institutions of the Church which did not enjoy specific sanction from the Bible. Well-wishers of Luther who were watching the spectacle with bated breath could not but see in his present position an ominous foreboding because these were the very same grounds on which the Czech reformer John Huss had been burned at the stake. In hindsight we can safely infer that Luther, in all likelihood, escaped a similar fate owing to the support he received from the Elector and the upsurge of German nationalistic fervour in support of his views which in its turn strengthened the Elector's hand. It must have become abundantly clear to Frederick that in the present situation the mood of the nation would not countenance any violent or precipitous action against Luther. The Leipzig debate unequivocally announced that Luther's intention now was a thorough cleansing, in root and branch, of the Catholic Church. As a consequence of his continual refusal to repudiate and recant what Rome had adjudged heretical in his written and spoken words, he was threatened with excommunication[15] and put under the papal ban by the papal bull[16] *Exsurge Domine* ('Arise Lord', echoing the opening words of psalm 68) of June 1520. In this exigency Staupitz released Luther from his monastic vows. In August of the same year there appeared Luther's counter-blast to Rome, *To the Christian Nobility of the German Nation*.

By now Luther may have had no mental misgivings about the gravity of the cause he championed and the dire

---

[15] Excommunication entailed severe penalties, such as the denial of the sacraments and fellowship of the church.

[16] A papal decree is called a bull after the seal (*bulla* in Latin) it bears. Its initial words serve as its title.

situation in which he had placed himself. Still, though fully aware of the mortal peril in which he stood, his conscience would not let him either to retract his words or retreat from his stand. However, one cannot but be struck by the irony of it all. What had set out probably as nothing more than an attempt on the part of a young scholar and academic to provoke a rational and informed discourse on what he saw as an abuse within the Church that ought to be eradicated or at least curtailed, now loomed so large in the nation's conscience as to invite the serious attention not only of the Church but of the secular powers also. Matters were swiftly moving and heading towards a crisis. Against the efforts of the Curia to have him extradited to Rome to stand trial as a heretic, Luther was invited to attend the Imperial Diet[17] at Worms. Thus the protracted legal and ecclesiastical proceedings against him culminated in a climax when he rose to defend his stand in the presence of the newly elected emperor Charles V with a whole host of other dignitaries, both temporal and religious. No real breakthrough could be achieved at the Diet because instead of the accused being given a chance to explain and vindicate his stand, he was again asked in plain terms simply to repudiate his writings. Now that he had alienated both the civil and ecclesiastical authorities, he was now fully and painfully cognizant of the dire consequences of his refusal to recant, that the fatal blow of both Church and state would fall upon his head. Yet, in ringing tones reminiscent of the defence of many a Christian martyr in times past, Martin defended himself. Here is what he said: "Since then your serene Majesty and your Lordships seek a simple answer, I will give it in this manner: Unless I am convinced by the testimony of the Scriptures or by clear reason (for I do not trust either in the Pope or in councils alone, since it is well known that they

---

[17] Diet: The meeting of the general assembly of the estates of the Holy Roman Empire. (The Holy Roman Empire was a Germanic empire located in central Europe.)

have often erred and contradicted themselves), I am bound by the Scriptures I have quoted and my conscience is captive to the Word of God. I cannot and I will not retract anything, since it is neither safe nor right to go against conscience. May God help me. Amen." With the emperor rescinding the safe conduct which afforded him relative safety, and the swift promulgation of the Edict of Worms, he was now virtually an outlaw before the civil authorities and a branded heretic in the eyes of the Church. In these dire straits Luther was secretly conveyed to Wartburg Castle where he lived, under the protection of Elector Frederick, incommunicado, under the assumed name of Junker Jorg.

The Luther Bible

In this self-imposed isolation and exile, Luther turned his leisure to the most productive and creative work of his lifetime, the translation of the Bible into the German[18] language. The debt that the modern German language owes to the Luther Bible is incalculable. We shall form some notion of the historical importance of the work if we remember that the language of the Church, the universities and indeed of all educated people all over Europe at that time and for generations afterwards was Latin. As far as the Germans were concerned, North and South Germans spoke completely different dialects which were mutually unintelligible. The High German (*Neuhochdeutsch*) dialect that Luther chose, in time, became the standard medium of German language and German literature. Honed and perfected by years of preaching, teaching and writing, Luther's language has the force of direct human speech. No one using the German language today can remain indifferent to Luther's linguistic legacy. The German New Testament—based on Erasmus's Greek New Testament—appeared in 1522. However, at the time the translation remained anonymous. By now Luther had left Wartburg Castle and gone back to Wittenberg where

---

[18] Germans call their language Deutsch.

he began the translation of the Old Testament which was finally finished in 1534. The Luther Bible was extremely popular and it is no exaggeration to say that it transformed German society as no other single work has done before or since. It is estimated that in the translator's lifetime alone there appeared no fewer than 377 editions.

Even at the risk of appearing distractingly digressive, some comments regarding the more modern translations and criticisms of the Bible seem to be in order at this stage. Contrary to the practice of many translators, critics and commentators, who in their superior wisdom take pride in tampering with the text in suggesting transposition or emendation of passages, it is a relief to turn to Luther who accepts the given text handed down by tradition (what in scholarly parlance is known as *textus receptus* or 'received text') and works on its basis. The outcome is a product of fidelity to its original and one of superior craftsmanship. On the other hand, in their zeal to improve matters, many a critic and translator instead of improving matters has only succeeded in leaving the text mangled and in disarray. Let me now commend to these over-zealous critics the sage advice of Samuel Johnson who in the course of his monumental edition of the complete plays of Shakespeare concluded that the wisest course was to leave the text unchanged. "As I practised conjecture more, I learned to trust it less; and after I had printed a few plays, resolved to insert none of my own readings in the text. Upon this caution I now congratulate myself, for every day increases my doubt of my emendations." Instead of improvement, what we are left with at the hands of many a Bible critic is uncertainty and confusion. Even when improvements are effected, they are generally marginal and are achieved at great loss of real pleasure and aesthetic enjoyment that great writing is intended to provide. Despite the availability today of more accurate manuscript text, more than one English translation leaves me with the thought that far from producing a version better than the King James, it is faulty and deficient at least here and there. The more I dip into the recent English versions, the more I am convinced of the virtues of the King James. Of course, linguistic change over the past four centuries calls for vigilance not to be led astray by words which have altered their meaning or at least their nuances. But the serious Bible reader should not be deterred by such a circumstance. There is an excellent resource in the Oxford English Dictionary, the only dictionary that I know that is built on historical principles. For lexical items that may have changed in course of time the OED supplies citations from writers contemporaneous with Jacobean times. The King James Bible will for ever remain a classic of English literature, unexcelled for its simplicity, elegance and euphonious rhythms. Any day I would rather be in the company of a great classic rather than with lesser entities. The New King James is well worth a try.

The lamp lit by Luther in making the Bible available to the common man in his native language inspired corresponding endeavours in several other European languages. We have already touched upon the path-breaking effort of John Wycliffe. However, the printed complete Wycliffe Bible did not appear till 1850 when the Oxford University Press published it. The important pioneering effort of William Tyndale and Miles Coverdale did eventually bear fruit in the magnificent classic, the Authorized or King James Version. Within a short period the Bible in the vernacular version appeared in France, Hungary, Denmark, Sweden, Poland, Finland and Iceland. All these translations owe not a little to Erasmus' magisterial Greek New Testament. Neither should we neglect to mention the work of the Hebraists. Between them and Erasmus an authentic and reliable text of the Old and the New Testaments was available ready to hand for the translators. The national Bibles profoundly transformed European society and culture by making Bible reading, study and devotion an important part of individual, familial and community life.

The Birth of Protestantism

It is high time we got back to Luther's life. As has already been mentioned, on leaving the Wartburg in March 1522, he went back to Wittenberg. The real birth of Protestantism as a religious movement with a marked identity of its own can be dated from 1522. In *The Pagan Servitude of the Church* Luther had set himself firmly against all manner of publicly established and instituted votive vows in the medieval Church, although he was not against individuals taking such vows. His main contention was that there was no Scriptural sanction for the imposition of the monastic vows of celibacy, poverty and obedience in religious institutions. Luther boldly pronounced that, in God's sight, the life of a monk, nun or priest was in no way superior to that of a farmer toiling on his farm or of a housewife taking care of her home and family. What really counted in the life of a Christian was faith alone. Luther's staunch stand against votive life caused quite a sensation all over Europe. As a consequence of the ferment, in religious foundations all across Germany, there started an exodus of monks and nuns. Forsaking their religious vows, they deserted their sequestered and cloistered lives and opted to join the larger Christian community. This period coincided with the birth of the reformed church in Zurich initiated and inspired by Zwingli.

Meanwhile Luther embarked on a tour of the Electorate of Saxony to propagate his beliefs on Christian doctrine and his views on worship and church organization. The order of worship in the reformed churches engaged his special attention. In the Catholic Church, music, indeed, played a prominent place. But the singing had been mostly, if not wholly, a monopoly of the choir with little or no participation by the congregation at large. It was due to Luther's initiative that today in the world-wide Christian communion congregational singing is the norm rather than the exception. It was to encourage the practice of congregational singing that he began to write hymns. The young Martin had been gifted with a great singing voice. A great lover of music, in youth he had learnt to play the lute and could improvise tunes and compose music. It was therefore inevitable that music would play an important role in the reformed religion. Luther tirelessly laboured on reforming the liturgy and in composing hymns meant for congregational singing. If today there is greater lay participation not only in singing but also in the service of worship we owe it to the legacy laid down by Luther. When this change began to occur it was a wholly new departure from the older order which had prevailed in the Catholic Church for centuries. Luther composed many hymns such as "Out of the depths I cry unto thee" (based on psalm 130), and "From heaven above to earth I come." Out of all the hymns that Luther wrote, in its original German version the hymn *Ein Feste Burg* is the best-loved and the most widely-known. Indeed it became a sort of battle cry among the masses of the Reformation Movement. It has been translated into many of the world's languages. In English it is available in two versions, both equally popular. "A mighty fortress is our God", a version translated by the American Frederick Hedge is perhaps the version one hears more often. The other translation by Thomas Carlyle has as its opening bar "A safe stronghold our God is still". One can hear the tune *"Ein Feste Burg"* being iterated in Felix Mendelssohn's[19] "Reformation Symphony". The opening line of the hymn is inscribed on Luther's tomb in Wittenberg. All in all, the contribution of German Protestantism to music is very substantial and transformational.

With the rapid strides that the Reformation ideals were making not only in the German lands but in other parts of Europe too, the most important phase of Luther's career may be reckoned to have come to an end. What remains of his life can now be set down in brief. With the induction of the versatile Philip Melanchthon, distinguished for his

---

[19] Felix Mendelssohn (1809-1847), German pianist, composer and conductor, was instrumental in reviving the music of J. S. Bach.

scholarship in both Greek and Hebrew, Luther acquired an able coadjutor and the reform movement a great leader and a capable organizer. He gave definition and clarity to points of doctrine fundamental to the Reformation. However, it was not all smooth sailing. There were serious setbacks too. The fresh wind of liberty blowing through the German lands stirred up some untoward events which seriously and at times even violently disturbed the social fabric. The Peasants Revolt for the restoration of their ancient rights which began in 1524 in the Black Forest region, gained fresh fuel from other disgruntled elements of German society and then the conflagration began to spread rapidly throughout the region. The leaders of the upheaval thought that it was a natural and direct expression of the new liberal ideals and liberating ideas circulating in the country and as a natural and logical extension of the fresh wind of change that was blowing through the German lands. The writings of Luther which had been their inspiration led them to look up to him as a staunch ally. However in the end they were left sorely disillusioned. Although Luther sympathized with some of their genuine grievances and demands for their redress, he felt that in the main, he could not support them as he believed that his views and principles had been distorted and perverted by certain zealots and anarchists among their leaders for their own selfish ends. The truth is that his innate conservative temperament and reverence for the old order were revolted as the eruption descended into violence and slaughter. His counsel to the insurgents to call off the agitation, obey their civil masters and resume their peaceful life naturally fell on deaf ears. During a tour of Thurangia when he personally witnessed the violence, arson, looting and bloodshed that the marauding mobs had committed he was greatly alarmed and appalled. Chagrined and exasperated, in his pamphlet "Against the Murderous, Thieving Hordes of Peasants" he called upon the political masters of the country to crush the revolt with a heavy hand. Grounding his arguments solidly on the Bible he reminded the civil authorities that it was their God-given duty to maintain order by putting down the rebellion. At the same time he reminded the rebels that it was their Christian duty to obey their masters as all authority is ordained by God. After much bloodshed and chaos gradually comparative calm and normalcy were restored. Luther's uncompromising stand against the rebellion, as might well have been anticipated, negatively impacted his standing and popularity among the masses.

One of the social consequences of Luther's reform programme was the challenge it posed to the Catholic Church's uncompromising policy of clerical celibacy. Although nurtured in the matrix of Judaism in which a numerous progeny was viewed as a sign of divine favour and celibacy was an uncommon exception, probably from the personal example of Jesus and his endorsement of those who chose to be eunuchs for the sake of the kingdom of God, the Church from early days regarded the single state as nobler and more honourable than the married one. Even Paul's attitude to the wedded state was rather as a concession to the weak-willed as his words "it is better to marry than to burn [with lust]" would seem to imply. No doubt the expectation of the Lord's imminent Advent would have weighed heavily in his mind in making the judgement. Anyway, with the ideas of reform filtering down among the people of Western Europe, priests, monks and nuns in droves abandoned their vows to embrace the wedded state and to raise families. Among many other innovations, Luther can legitimately be called the creator of the Protestant parsonage. Though doctrinally inclined to support the wedded state for the religious, Luther himself was averse from embarking on matrimony chiefly from the looming threat of instant assassination by virtue of his being a heretic before the Church and an outlaw in the eyes of the state. However, a tricky and delicate dilemma developed when nuns in a neighbouring village left their cloisters on his advice. When domestic care was secured either as wives or housekeepers for all but one, Luther felt personally responsible for her rehabilitation. To cut a long story short, finally on June 13, 1525 Catherine von Bora, who had not been otherwise properly provided for, became his wife. Luther's initial reluctance was overcome when he felt that his marriage, besides being a testimony to his personal faith in the sanctity of the wedded state, would please his father who had been urging him to marry and continue the family line. Elector Frederick bestowed on the couple the Augustinian monastery called the Black Cloister for their residence. Catherine proved to be an efficient manager of her household and the Luthers saw many years of domestic felicity.

Meanwhile the reform movement, despite setbacks, continued its unhindered and unrelenting progress. In October 1529 Philip I, the 'Landgrave'[20] of the German State of Hesse convened a Colloquium of German and Swiss Protestant theologians at Marburg with a view to formulating a doctrinal consensus among the various Protestant states. This landmark event known as the Marburg Colloquy was attended, besides Luther, by Zwingli, Melanchthon and a number of other leading Protestant thinkers and theologians. Although agreement was reached on almost all matters of doctrine and belief, no unanimity on the vital question of the Communion could be arrived at. Indeed, what became crystal clear at the Colloquy was that there seemed to be as many differing subtle nuances on the real significance and meaning of Lord's Supper as there were participants! Howbeit, there did emerge two central points of divergence. The vast majority regarded the Lord's Supper as no more than a sacred memorial to Christ's redeeming sacrifice. In any case most of the leaders could not go beyond the belief in the Lord's spiritual and symbolic presence in the sacrament. Luther, on the other hand, although fundamentally opposed to the Roman doctrine of transubstantiation, would not

---

[20] Landgrave: The title of a Count having jurisdiction over a large territory in Medieval Germany.

swerve from his entrenched belief in the real presence of Christ in the elements. Ultimately, failing to achieve unanimity of views on the Lord's Supper, the participants of the Colloquy decided to leave matters alone.

With key points in the new Protestant creed now largely settled, during a tour of Saxony with fellow-workers, the reformed church service was inaugurated. In the course of this itinerary it dawned on Luther that there was a categorical imperative to impart instruction in the fundamentals of Protestantism to its new adherents. The 'Large Catechism'[21] that he compiled in this context was used for the instruction and training of pastors and teachers and it did produce a large corps of educated and well-trained leaders. Though on similar lines and meant to serve much the same purpose, the 'Small Catechism' was intended for the training of lay members of the various congregations. Despite their differing emphases both Catechisms had a large body of common material comprising a conspectus of the Ten Commandments, the Apostles' Creed, the Lord's Prayer, and the Protestant teaching regarding baptism and the Lord's Supper. As a compact codification of the new Protestant faith Luther's catechisms remain classics of their kind. Meanwhile, the liturgy as well as the manner and the order in which the divine service was conducted also underwent major changes. The 'German Mass' that Luther composed soon replaced the Roman Catholic Mass in the newly erected Protestant churches although the substantive difference between them was slight, but for the exclusion in the German Mass of the notion that the Mass was a re-enactment of Christ's sacrifice on the cross. Nevertheless, Luther's insistence that the Last Supper was never intended by Christ to take the place of His impending sacrifice and that therefore the Communion was not a sacrifice but a fellowship of believers drastically changed its nature. The worshipper was

---

[21] A Catechism is a treatise for instruction in the elements of the Christian religion, usually in the form of questions and answers.

now free to drink the wine and take the bread in his hands and participate in the Communion without priestly confession. This change marked an extremely important departure from the Roman Catholic position. We will do well to recall that the Catholic Church had denied the communicant participation in the second element of the sacrament. Yet another salutary outcome of the Reformation was that the sermon came to occupy a central role in church worship. So also did music in the form of congregational singing and recitation in unison of the creed and the liturgy. On the whole, gradually, lay members of the congregation took over from the clergy at least some more of the functions which had been the preserve of the priests. These included not only playing a more important role in worship but also in church administration.

With the reformed churches moving swiftly apace with their innovative practices, there was little chance of working out an accommodation with the Catholic Church. Yet the Holy Roman Emperor, a staunch Catholic hoped to use the looming threat to the peace of Europe from the depredations of the Turk to seek a working compromise. In 1530 with the Turks laying siege to Vienna, Emperor Charles V convened an imperial Diet at Augsburg to work out a rapprochement between the Roman Catholic and Protestant positions. Since the imperial interdiction on Luther was still in force and no safe conduct to travel to Augsburg could be procured he was represented at the Diet by Melanchthon. The 'Augsburg Confession', largely the work of this distinguished scholar and theologian was rejected by Charles as well as by the Catholic Church. Despite the Diet's apparent failure, the next year the leading Protestant states, with the exception of the Protestant autonomous city states of Switzerland, came together to form the Schmalkad League.

Meanwhile Luther suffered a major illness in 1537 while he was in Schmalkad working on what is known as the 'Schmalkad Articles'. As the years passed by he suffered bouts of depression and a series of intermittent periods of ill-health. However by now the major goals of his life's mission had been well and truly won. Slowly but steadily Protestant churches started springing up in several countries, mainly in Western Europe. His last important piece of writing was the 'Short Confession' on the Lord's Supper (1546). Years of confrontation with the Catholic Church, bitter exchanges in theological controversies, his unremitting labour over his numerous publications, his ceaseless toil in launching the new reform movement and organizing the reformed churches and their services had all sapped his energies. His achievements, though momentous and monumental had finally taken their toll. In January 1546, accompanied by his sons, he travelled to Eisleben for the last time. Universally hailed as the prince of preachers, Luther had to his credit hundreds of sermons, his very last sermon being given just a few days before his death. Providentially the end came when he was involved in a delicate peace mission. Despite failing health, he went to Eisleben to settle a dispute between two brothers belonging to the noble house of the counts of Mansfeld. Luther died on the way back home, but one feels sure, with the gratifying sensation that he had brought about reconciliation between the warring brothers. He was buried under the pulpit of the Castle Church in Wittenberg.

Chapter 5

LUTHER AND THE BIBLE: HIS DISCOVERY OF THE GOSPEL

The spark that lit the mighty conflagration called the Reformation that engulfed most of Europe within a brief spell was Luther's intense love affair with the Bible. Incredible as it may sound, it nevertheless remains true, that, as has been hinted at earlier, at the time the Bible was little known even among the religious orders and the clergy. What caused this abysmal ignorance of and indifference to the Bible even among those who chose to follow the Church was the lopsided vision that gave prominence to the interpretation of the scriptures by medieval schoolmen rather than to the direct study of the text of the Bible. Sadly, instead of focussing on Biblical revelation, medieval churchmen concerned themselves rather with its exegesis by scholastic theologians such as Thomas Aquinas, Duns Scotus and William of Occam.[1] As has been pointed out by Luther himself in his "Preface to the Psalms" the favoured topics of study in the monasteries and other religious foundations of the day were legends of saints and Passionals, i.e., accounts of the life and sufferings of saints. These were supplemented by books of edification and moral stories. To medieval churchmen the *Sententia (Sentences)* of Peter Lombard,[2] comprising a selection from Scriptures, Patristic writings and

---

[1] William of Occam (1290-1349) was an English scholastic philosopher and theologian. He was a pupil of Duns Scotus. He joined the Franciscan order and became its general in 1342. In his *Dialogus* he contested the temporal power of the pope and asserted the king's power in civil affairs.

[2] Peter Lombard (c.1100-c.1164), Italian scholastic theologian, is often called *Magister Sententiarum* (Master of the Sentences). The compilation is made up of quotations from Church authorities on matters of doctrine and the sayings of the Church Fathers.

LUTHER AND THE BIBLE: HIS DISCOVERY OF THE GOSPEL   69

the Scholastics, constituted the cream of theology. This curriculum constituted the core of theological learning in the medieval university too. The Bible was but seldom looked at as a record of divine revelation and studied for its own sake as the Word of God. Where it was attempted as by Thomas Aquinas in his monumental *Summa Theologica* and other works, Holy Writ was perceived refracted through the prism of Aristotelian dialectics. Augustine of Hippo's illuminating insights which led to his dramatic and historic conversion[3] to Christianity had all but been forgotten through neglect. It remained for the Augustinian monk Luther to rediscover the Bible and look at it afresh as a record of a divine revelation as to how sinful humanity could attain salvation.

Despite his having been a rather typical product of the medieval system of philosophical and religious education and training in which the textual study of the Bible did not enjoy pride of place, Luther was led to a serious exploration of the mystery of the sacred Scriptures. As it happily turned out, as if by divine design, in Johannes Staupitz, the Superior of his monastery, he did find a beneficent beacon. Unlike the typical monk of the time, Staupitz knew what a precious treasure the Bible was, as in it lay locked the secret of salvation. Convinced of its supreme importance, he instituted the serious study of the Bible in his monastery. The inspiration behind Luther's life-long and serious engagement with the Word of God was none other than his mentor Staupitz. To repeat what has been stated earlier in another context, Staupitz' enthusiasm for fostering Biblical study and knowledge was so great that when in 1502 the Elector Frederick the Wise of Saxony asked him to found a university in Wittenberg, the latter instituted a professorship of the Bible there, a rather unique position in any university at the time. Although Staupitz himself occupied the position to

---

[3] *The Confessions* of Aurelius Augustine is one of the great classics of Christian meditative literature.

begin with, it was later transferred to Luther, a circumstance that led to his total immersion in Biblical studies.

Luther has successfully plumbed the very depths and brought up before us the uniqueness of the mystery of the Gospel of Jesus Christ as no one else has done, it seems to me. He has indeed discovered a pearl of great price in the Word of God and displayed its luminous light forcefully and powerfully before our wondering eyes. Whereas the Elder Luther spent his life digging up copper ore from the bowels of the earth, his illustrious son busied himself bringing up nuggets of gold from the treasury of God's precious Word. Continuous poring over the varied books of the Bible has enabled him to expound the mystery of God's revelation to future generations. Despite his profound scholarship in philosophy and religion, he makes no attempt to tinker with the text as many Biblical scholars deficient in the historical imagination tend to do. With deep reverence Luther receives the text as it is handed down by generations of God's faithful people. His entire focus is to glean from its pages dazzling gems of spiritual truths and wisdom. In his lectures and prefaces to the various books of the Bible, he is entirely successful in forging a style that has the beauty of simplicity and elegance in order to display with consummate mastery his ware of spiritual truths before his readers. Therefore it is indeed worth our while to take a detailed look at his lectures and commentaries.

Luther's continual and sustained interest in St. Paul's Epistle to the Galatians—he had earlier lectured on Galatians in 1519 and 1513—points to the centrality it occupies in the progress and development of his theology based solely on faith. In his "Commentary on Galatians" of 1531 we find him delving deeper into the heart and mind of Paul. For one thing we are now provided with the clearest exposition of his fully-wrought reflections on the polarity between the Gospel and the Law. The present treatise is equally significant for its systematic development of the doctrine of justification by faith that is the bedrock of the Protestant credo. He sets down the theme of the Epistle as Paul's theology concerning

Christian faith. Further he fully defines and then elaborately explains the doctrine of Christian righteousness and differentiates it from other forms of righteousness such as political, civil and ceremonial righteousness. Christian righteousness differs from all others in the sense that at the heart of it lies God's forgiveness of our sins through His grace based solely on our faith in Christ.

The Preface to Luther's translation of the New Testament is a veritable gold mine of Biblical insights. He views the Old Testament basically as a volume containing God's laws and commandments. Further it records the history of those who kept His laws and commandments and those who failed to keep them. Clearly he sets much greater score on the New Testament. His extraordinary insight into the core of Biblical truth lies open before us when he proclaims that the entire Bible — the Old and the New Testaments taken in their totality — constitutes a single Gospel, the *Via Salvatore*, the Way of Salvation. Quintessentially viewed, the good news that the Word of God proclaims is salvation story. Although the integral Bible points directly to Jesus and the royal road to freedom from sin that He has opened up to sinful humanity through His sacrifice, specifically, it is in the New Testament that God's promised *evangel* is enclosed. "*Evangel* is a Greek word meaning glad tidings, good news, welcome information, a shout, or something that makes one sing and talk and rejoice" (Luther, "Preface to New Testament," Dillenberger, p.115). Luther further clarifies that the Gospel of Jesus is indeed a war-cry, a shout of triumph, similar to David's victorious shout when he defeated Goliath. Jesus Christ's good news, the same triumphal cry would soon be heard reverberating throughout the world in the mission of His apostles. Fortified and filled with the spirit of the risen Lord, they travelled far and wide proclaiming how Jesus, the true David, rode victorious over sin, death and the devil.

Moreover, to make the point doubly clear Luther goes on to explain that the *evangel* is like a man's last will and testament in which he bequeaths his estate to his heirs.

After gaining victory over sin and death by means of His sacrifice, in the New Testament, which is Christ's last will and testament, He imparts to all believers His life, righteousness and holiness. The full force of Luther's exposition of Christ's evangel can best be rendered in his own idiom.

> God's evangel, the New Testament, is a good piece of news, a war-cry.... This kind of war-cry, this heartening news, this evangelical, divine message, is called a new testament. It is also like a testament when a dying man decides how his property shall be divided among certain heirs, whom he names. In the same way, Christ, before His death, decided and commanded that this evangel was to be proclaimed to all the world after His death. He thereby gave all believers possession of all His goods: namely, His life, by which He had vanquished death; His righteousness, by which He had washed away sin; and His holiness, by which He had overcome eternal damnation. (Luther, "Preface to New Testament," Dillenberger, p.15).

In the same document Luther goes on to aver that, equally, the Bible is a veritable record of God's manifold promises. One of the earliest recorded promises of Almighty God that the seed of the woman shall bruise the devil's heel (Genesis 3:15) comes to fruition when Christ, the seed of the woman, tramples down sin, death and hell, all of which evils emanate from the devil's head. It is solely through the seed of the woman, the Incarnation of God in Jesus Christ, His subsequent loving immolation and His eventual glorious resurrection which have opened up for us the escape route from sin, death and hell. Luther goes on to demonstrate further on in the same treatise how God's promise to Abraham that in his seed shall all the nations of the earth be blessed (Genesis 22:18) too is fulfilled in Jesus Christ, the seed of Abraham (Galatians 3:16). All who believe in Christ through His gospel shall be reckoned as righteous and shall live with Him for ever, delivered from sin, death and hell. Yet another of the Almighty's promises, this time made to David (II Kings: 17) that his kingdom will last for ever too is fulfilled in Christ. That kingdom is the kingdom of Christ proclaimed in the gospel, an eternal kingdom of life, blessedness, and righteousness that lies open to all those who trust and believe in Jesus Christ. All those who repose their unfeigned trust in Christ are loosed for ever from the bonds of sin and death.

The Preface to the Luther New Testament is an invaluable treasury of Biblical insights. It is in it that we come across the key to the sinner's salvation which ultimately resounded as the creed of the Reformation faith, namely that it is achievable by faith alone (*sola fide*). It powerfully and vehemently affirms that works are of no avail in redeeming us from the shackles of sin and eventual death. Salvation has already been procured for us by Christ by His redeeming sacrifice. His work, namely His passion and death, makes us righteous and gives us life and salvation.

Yet another substantial document in coming to terms with the Reformation credo is Luther's Preface to the Epistle to the Romans. As it happened with Augustine of Hippo, so it was to Martin Luther also that it was Paul's Epistle to the Romans that opened to him the portals to Paradise. Therefore a careful look at it is bound to reward us with rich spiritual dividends. A paean of praise for the Epistle meets us as we begin our perusal of the Preface. Luther exhorts us to meditate on this veritable gospel according to Paul day by day and urges us even to learn it by heart as it enshrines the good news of Jesus in its purest form. In the Epistle to the Romans we come across a reiterated emphasis on faith rather than on meritorious works. Luther is quick to point out that faith is not dependent on man's volition, but that it is God's gratuitous gift. Faith itself is the fruit of the Word of God, the Gospel, and it is faith that leads to good works. It is impossible for man to attain righteousness, to become right with God, by means of meritorious works. On the contrary, it is solely by virtue of a new spiritual birth, in faith we become partakers and inheritors of Christ's righteousness. The grace of God, the unearned favour of God, is sufficient to enable us to be accounted entirely and completely righteous in His sight.

By no means was Luther's interest in the Bible confined to the New Testament. Assuredly, the Book of Psalms must have been one of Luther's all-time favourites, judging by the frequency with which he lectured and commented upon it and by the quality of the penetrating and original remarks he made on it. Therefore by all accounts his "Preface to the Psalms" is well worth a close look. He calls the Book of Psalms a miniature Bible, a sort of microcosm of the Bible. According to him it sets out in the briefest and most beautiful form all that is found in the whole of the Bible. The Book of Psalms is unique in the sense that it furnishes us with a record of what the saints of the Old Testament said and did, how they communed with God and prayed to Him. In the psalms the saints of the Old Testament appear before us alive and in the round. Their deepest and noblest utterances in the very act of communing and communicating with God are preserved intact and in toto in these noble songs. The psalmists lay bare before us their hearts and the deepest treasures hidden in their hearts in these their heart-felt utterances. The Psalms enable us to peep into their very hearts and minds as they confronted the storms of life. They touch upon the entire gamut of human emotions ranging from paeans of praise to Almighty God as in the Hallel Psalms and careering through the heights of our earthly joys to the depths of human sorrow and misery as in the penitential psalms and the psalms of lamentation. So comprehensive is their range that the chances are that we shall find in the corpus apt ones to suit our every individual and particular spiritual need. The very same words used by the psalmists to commune with God shall come in handy on our part to talk to God.

Luther's Biblical corpus is too voluminous for us to review in its totality. I suppose a sufficient sampling has been presented to give the reader its rare flavour and to whet his appetite for further experimentation and experience its richness on his own. It is time we turned to some other of Luther's major writings.

Chapter 6

LUTHER'S OTHER MAJOR WRITINGS

Solidly anchored on the core teaching of Jesus and the Apostles in the New Testament, in a series of writings Luther systematically enunciated the tenets on which the Church of Christ ought to be founded. Among these are *The Freedom of a Christian* (1520), *The Pagan Servitude of the Church* (commonly called *The Babylonian Captivity of the Church*), and *An Appeal to the Ruling Class* (1520). In an open letter to Pope Leo X which forms a sort of a foreword to the *Freedom of a Christian*, Luther clarified that his animadversions were not aimed at the person of the pope. On the other hand, his ire was turned against the corrupt practices and ungodly doctrines which had tainted the good name of the papacy. The real administrator of papal power and privilege, namely the Roman Curia, was mired in miserable corruption and godless licentiousness. Luther believed that his righteous indignation against this den of thieves was thoroughly justified.

Luther felt that the fundamental doctrines of the Church of Christ had been either subverted or relegated to the background in the practice of the medieval Catholic Church. What had happened in the previous few centuries was that their rightful place had been taken over by routine rites, rituals and ceremonies. What he now sought to accomplish through his radical propositions was to recover, re-formulate and re-define the dogmas of the Apostolic Church, Scripture alone serving as the foundation on which the new Reformation faith was going to be built. As he gave full and concrete expression to his reformation programme by word of mouth through his sermons and in his writings, it soon became apparent to Luther and his followers that a complete severance from the older faith was inevitable. Having penetrated the mystery of the Word of God Luther was not going to be swayed by the thunder and lightning emanating from the pope and the Curia. The pristine purity, holiness and simplicity of the first Christian community would be the guiding lights of the new ecclesia. What were the major departures and differences that marked Martin Luther's newfound enlightenment?

The initial salvo against the Church of Rome was fired against the institution of the Mass, the beliefs surrounding it and the manner in which it was being administered in the contemporary Roman Catholic Church. Luther was fully cognizant of the fact that the Mass constituted the cornerstone of the Catholic faith. If today the specific institution of the Mass is celebrated only by Roman Catholic priests and it is variously called the Communion, the Holy Communion, the Lord's Supper, the Lord's Table, the Eucharist, by the various Protestant denominations, we owe this change, not only as regards its nomenclature, but also to our faith and practice regarding it to none other than this German reformer. What Luther has done was to go back to the faith and practice as regards the establishment and administration of the sacrament as recorded in the Bible. What can be affirmed unequivocally and categorically is that it is a sacrament instituted by Jesus Himself. The clearest and fullest account of it is found in Luke 22:14-20. In verse 19 we find a specific commandment to observe the love fest as a perennial memorial of Christ's redemptive sacrifice. The corresponding narrative in Matthew occurs in Matthew 26:26-29. Although the call to observe it as a commemoration of the cross is not specifically spelt out there, would not the sheer poignancy of the words of Jesus and their heartrending context make it incumbent on the disciples to do so? Would not a believer inescapably associate the image of Christ's broken body and spilt blood on the cross with the Communion? An amplified account of the institution of the Eucharist occurs in Paul's letter to the Christian congregation in the Greek city of Corinth (1 Corinthians 11: 23-29). In all probability what we do get in this passage is a description of how the Lord's Supper was celebrated in the primitive church. Moreover, verses 26-29 throw some light on how Paul viewed the sacrament and personally participated and partook in it and how deep a spiritual experience it was to him. In the apostle's personal faith regarding it and in his individual practice did he invest the rite with an added spiritual aura and mystique?

Luther's clearest exposition of the observance is found in the *Pagan Servitude of the Church* (also called the *Babylonian Captivity of the Church*). What he set out to do in this publication was to develop a Biblical and Reformation conception of the sacraments and of the Church based solidly on Scripture alone and to demonstrate how far the Roman Church had diverged from the Apostolic Church's faith and practice. Specifically, this document was penned to counter Rome's practice of withholding the cup from the laity in the administration of the Mass. At the time in the service of the Mass only the priests were permitted to drink the wine. It is possible that the restriction might have been necessitated out of fear that some clumsy layman might spill some of the wine after it had been transubstantiated to Christ's blood. In Luther's treatise he takes us back to the institution of the solemn rite by the Lord Himself and reiterates that the substances used are real bread and real wine. Apparently, as affirmed by Luther, during the first twelve centuries of the Christian era there was not even a hint of transubstantiation[1] in connection with the Mass. The early Patristic writings do not contain even an isolated reference to it. Hence Luther has no hesitation in unambiguously asserting that it is a wholly human invention altogether unsupported by Scripture.

---

[1] Transubstantiation is the belief that the elements, the bread and the wine are transformed into the flesh and the blood of Jesus Christ.

Luther now points an accusatory finger at Thomas Aquinas for letting this misleading teaching creep into the faith and practice of the Catholic Church in the course of this Church Father's gigantic intellectual tour de force of working out a synthetic philosophical system by reconciling Biblical revelation with Aristotle's philosophy. The following, in a nutshell, is how the Angelic Doctor worked out his theory of transubstantiation on which the Roman Church's doctrine regarding this sacrament is vested. Aquinas clarifies that while the elements of bread and wine retained their *accidents* of shape, colour, taste, etc. they lost their *substance* and were transmuted into the substance of God. With the indoctrination of the notion that the transubstantiation of the elements of bread and wine was central to the observance of the Mass, what had been administered as a holy sacrament in the previous thirteen-hundred years was sought to be turned into a sort of magical rite by the priestly celebrant of the Mass. A holy and blessed sacrament to memorialize the Lord's sacrifice had been, in the practice of the medieval Catholic Church, allowed to degenerate into a commodity in a marketplace, a business run for gain and that is what calls out Luther's righteous indignation.

From this distance of time the demand for Communion in both kinds may sound innocuous enough. But as far as the Catholic Church was concerned, Luther's call for communion in both kinds for the laity had an ominous ring about it as the very same demand had been made by the so-called heretic John Huss and his followers. Nor was the Mass the only institution that needed change according to Luther. All manner of other rites and ceremonies such as special feasts, anniversaries, memorial days, all of which had been let into the Church with official patronage through the back door with an eye for profit alone also needed to be ostracized and outlawed forthwith. Through the written medium what Luther endeavours to accomplish is to teach the truth regarding the Lord's Supper, stripping the sacrament of all the unwanted accretions which had accumulated around it in course of time. Moreover he wished to eliminate from this sacred memorial act all its external paraphernalia such as vestments, candles, ornaments, indeed, the whole set of pageantry associated with the Mass which he believed, are all human additions made in the past three centuries. Let us devote our minds, hearts and souls, he called on fellow-Christians, purely and simply to what Christ Himself had instituted.

The importance of this treatise by Luther cannot be overstated as in it he penetrates the heart of the mystery of the Lord's Supper. Guided by the light of the Gospel and inspired by the Holy Spirit he gives us a new insight into the observance when he characterises the sacrament of the Communion as Christ's last will and testament. It is instructive to follow each step of Luther's as he works out his argument. His discourse on the Lord's Supper has all the neatness of a logical syllogism. In view of His impending death, by means of this testament Jesus bequeaths His heritage and names His heirs. We are now referred to the narratives in the New Testament Epistles — specifically to Romans chapter 4, Galatians chapters 3 and 4 and Hebrews chapter 9 — wherein Paul discusses the subject threadbare. While the words of Jesus: "This is my blood which is shed" testifies to His own death, the words "for you and for many" serve to nominate the heirs. Finally, Jesus designates the bequest and clarifies that it is for "the remission of sins." The uniqueness of this mysterious transaction is this that, because the testator is God himself and God cannot die, the Incarnation was necessitated in order to achieve the Almighty's plan to redeem sinful humanity from the clutches of the Devil. Here in an original and the most profound way Luther effectively incorporates the Incarnation and the Resurrection in and through the Communion. In characterizing the poignant and pregnant words of Jesus at the Last Supper as His last will and testament, Luther has indeed revealed a fresh facet of this sacred ceremony and enabled us to experience some of its rich inner meaning and significance. When we participate in the Communion in full faith, Christ acknowledges our adoption as His heirs and bestows on us our patrimony which is salvation. The sum and substance of his detailed analysis is that for a worthy participation in the Lord's Supper, the one and only thing requisite is faith. Communion may be received trusting in Christ's promise alone and one's acceptance of it in faith. In the heat of the controversy and the Catholic Church's dogmatic insistence on the theory of transubstantiation, Luther may have veered to a polar opposite position on the subject. Yet it is important to reiterate that personally to Luther the Holy Communion was no mere reminder of Jesus' loving sacrifice. It was a profound spiritual event, a tremendous mystery, in which the communicant in a way that is hard to communicate experienced the real, albeit spiritual, presence of Christ. In theological parlance Luther's view regarding what the communicant experiences during the Communion is referred to as consubstantiation to differentiate it from transubstantiation. Incidentally, the non-Catholic Syrian Christian Churches of India such as the Orthodox, Jacobite and Mar Thoma Syrian Christians too traditionally adhere to the doctrine of consubstantiation.

It is time we looked at other major departures in the faith and practice of the reformed churches that flowed from Luther's writings. As far as the Catholic Church was concerned, the right observance of and adherence to the several sacraments played a vital role in presenting sinful man as a redeemed soul before God. The pivotal role of the clergy rested on the reality that the sacraments had to be mediated and administered solely through its agency. In the beginning most probably the Church observed but two sacraments which were regarded as essential, namely, baptism and Communion. But by medieval times their number had swelled to seven. With the rise in the number and importance of sacraments as means of grace, the power and influence of the clerical fraternity were naturally on the ascendant. However, the really deplorable thing about the administration of the sacraments was not only their quantitative rise but also their being bought and sold for money. Luther was naturally horrified and appalled by the spectacle of God's grace which was a free gift bestowed on every repentant sinner, being bartered for gold and silver through the shameless trade in sacraments. When brought face to face with this scandalous practice, it is no wonder that he set his face firmly against the evil. His poring over the Scriptures had led him to the conclusion that only two ceremonies deserved the distinction of being elevated to ecclesiastical sacraments. Since we have already looked at his views on the Mass there is no need to revisit the topic. Let us turn to Luther's views on baptism.

Regarding baptism too Luther forces us to go back to the Bible for a genuine understanding of the meaning and significance of the sacrament. Here he takes us back to the foundational statement of Jesus in a key verse found in Mark's gospel: "He that believeth and is baptized shall be saved" (Mark 16:16). Faith being the most excellent and the most difficult of all works, Luther calls upon his readers to pay the greatest attention to faith rather than stress the importance of the ritual as was the usual practice in his time. Though the Greek word *baptizo* – which occurs in the original Greek text – means to immerse or plunge, and *baptisma* literally means immersion, Luther was not personally opposed to the age-old and widespread practice of infant baptism observed alike in the Catholic and the Orthodox Churches. Although he was fully convinced that faith is the essential ingredient in this rite, he is equally and keenly alive to its symbolic significance. Luther unravels the full spiritual meaning of this hallowed ceremony when he points out how the death to sin and the rise to spiritual rebirth of the person baptized are both symbolized, as submersion signifies death while the lifting up of the subject signifies his resurrection. By means of the death and resurrection implied in baptism, a new creation, a re-generation, a spiritual birth, has occurred during the operation of this hallowed ceremonial.

Next Luther turns his attention to an inquiry into the institution of Christian marriage by proposing the moot question whether marriage is a sacrament or not. The Roman Church avows that it is and Luther with his insistence that there are only two genuine sacraments instituted by Jesus that are recorded in the Bible, namely Communion and baptism, denies that it is. As always, Luther turns to the Biblical text for guidance. When we get back to the original text in Greek, it says: "The twain shall become one flesh. This is a great mystery". In lieu of the Greek term *mysterion* (mystery), the Latin Vulgate text employs the expression *sacramentum* (sacrament). Apparently, this semantic slip resulted in the Catholic Church converting Christian marriage into one of the seven sacraments of the medieval Catholic Church. We may in this context do well to take a look at the Biblical narrative where Paul discusses Christian marriage. After quoting the relevant extract from Genesis 2:24, he writes: "This is a great mystery" and immediately hastens to add "I speak concerning Christ and the Church" (Ephesians 5:32). Like Paul, here again Luther unlocks a great mystery when he calls matrimony a sort of material allegory of the union of Christ and the Church which is the greater mystery. This mystery which surpasses our rational and intellectual understanding can perhaps be apprehended by faith alone.

At this juncture Luther exposes some of the evils which have gradually crept into the Catholic Church in the practical administration of the canon law pertaining to marriage. Luther, as ever, goes to the root of the problem when he says that the bond that joins man and woman in Christian matrimony is love and loving union is beyond and above man-made laws. Being a divine institution marriage ought not to be broken to conform to rules and regulations. Yet the oppressive rulers of the Roman Church, its priests and prelates, granted divorce to couples or enforced unions according to their whims and fancies and not according to the Scriptural tenets. In the practice of the contemporary Church union between a believer and a non-Christian was frowned upon. Luther now poses a pertinent question: should religious disparity between partners be an impediment to their coming together? He is of the firm conviction that such unions ought not to be forbidden because the early annals of the church point otherwise. He cites an outstanding example from past Church history. The pagan Patricius and the Christian Monica, were the parents of Augustine of Hippo. In Apostolic times when the Christian religion spread to the Gentile world such unequal union must have been fairly common. It is well worth listening to Paul's practical advice in such situations.

> If any brother hath a wife that believeth not, and she be pleased to dwell with him, let him not put her away. And the woman which hath an husband that believeth not, and if he be pleased to dwell with her, let her not leave him. For the unbelieving husband is sanctified by the wife, and the unbelieving wife is sanctified by the husband: else were your children unclean; but now are they holy (I Corinthians 7: 12-14).

It is high time, reminds Luther, that the Church restored to each and every Christian his God-given liberty.

One of the themes dear to Luther's heart and to which he devotes substantial space in his writings is the proper administration of the Christian Church as a whole on the one hand and its far-flung congregations on the other. So naturally the various offices of the Church and the services provided by it are of vital concern to him. He laments the present state of the Catholic Church administration and deplores the gulf that divides it from the practices that prevailed during the apostolic times. In criticizing the contemporary administration, the ideal he visualises is naturally first-century Christianity. One of the most radical innovations that the Reformation inaugurated was in regard to the Christian ministry. The so-called sacrament of ordination of priests was unknown to the primitive church. According to Luther it is a purely human institution invented by the Church Fathers. Like many other ceremonies inducted by the Church Fathers without Biblical sanction or precedence in the primitive Church, ordination too, Luther reiterates, is an ecclesiastical ceremony pure and simple. Once again taking his stand solely on evidence found in early Christianity, Luther now states his position that all baptized Christians are priests. What, he inquires next, is the primary task of a minister of the church? Early church history is explicit on the question that it is preaching the Word of God. In other words, Christian priests are chosen by the people to be "ministers of Christ and stewards of the mysteries of God" (I Corinthians 4:1). On this subject too Biblical evidence is wholly on the side of Luther. The New Testament Epistles in particular are replete with instances where all believers are routinely addressed as saints and priests. Against this backdrop Luther was strongly in favour of the Church redefining the role and functions of a minister of the church.

Other deviations and departures from the work of church leaders also received Luther's careful scrutiny. For example, the function of a deacon at the time contemporaneous with the Reformation was to read from the gospel or from one of the epistles. During apostolic times deacons were chosen to distribute the bounty of the Church to the poor so that the apostles could devote themselves to prayer and the preaching of the Word. Luther now makes a thorough examination of the manner in which the early Church was governed. Unlike the practice at the time, in the early church it was the leaders of the community who were elected as elders. Luther clarifies that they were chosen for their maturity and experience, and the selection was unaccompanied by any ritual either of ordination or consecration. This discussion actually spills over into Luther's next publication: *An Appeal to the Ruling Class* (1520).

From the foregoing discussion we should not jump to the hasty conclusion that Luther was indifferent to the solemnity and sanctity attached to the office of a minister of the Church. In order to forestall any such misgiving Luther asks: does it therefore follow that anyone can arbitrarily assume any office in the Church? His answer is a categorical negative. No election can be deemed to be valid and legal unless it receives the mandate of the congregation. From Church history he cites several examples such as those of Augustine, Ambrose and Cyprian and demonstrates that they were elected in this manner by the people to serve the community as bishops. Luther is firmly of the view that equity and fraternity should alone define all relationships in a Christian community because all of us are equal before God and therefore it is most unbecoming to maintain any form of hierarchy among the officers and leaders of the Church. In Luther's judgement every baptized Christian is fit to be consecrated priest, bishop or pope. But in so far as we possess different abilities and talents, we are called upon to undertake duties and responsibilities suited to our skills. Evidently this was the practice during apostolic times as can be inferred from Paul's writing.

> To one there is given through the Spirit the message of wisdom, to another the message of knowledge by means of the same Spirit, to another faith by the same Spirit, to another gifts of healing by that one Spirit, to another miraculous powers, to another prophecy, to another distinguishing between spirits, to another speaking in different kinds of tongues, and to still another the interpretation of tongues. All these are the work of one and the same Spirit and he gives them to each one, just as he determines (I Corinthians 12: 8-11; NIV).

Isn't it significant that in Paul's enumeration of the various offices and duties of Christians, priesthood is a notable omission?

It is instructive in this context to turn our attention to the rather elaborate disquisition on Christ's High Priestly role in the Epistle to the Hebrews. As the writer of this Epistle is eager to point out, the line of descent of His priesthood is not from Aaron, as Jesus belonged to the tribe of Judah and not of Levi. The fact of the matter is that the principal function of the priest in Jewish society was to offer sacrifices. The destruction of the Temple in A.D. 70 brought the sacrificial cult and along with it the Levitic priesthood to an end. The High Priest entered the Holy of Holies once a year to offer sacrifices on his behalf as well as the entire Jewish nation scattered world-wide. With the sacrifice of Christ for all time and for all humanity Jewish priesthood had been rendered redundant. As the writer of Hebrews is at pains to emphasize the High-Priesthood of Christ is after the manner of the mystery character Melchizedek. Rather it comes down from the Father's consecration of the Son through the Spirit. The Christian ministry clearly devolves from Jesus Christ and there is clear Biblical endorsement of Luther's position on the issue.

It is clear from the foregoing extract from one of the letters of Paul that the absence of class and hierarchy makes all Christians equal. Luther now appeals to the civil authorities to reform the Church and restrain its excessive powers. He tells them in no uncertain terms that the pope's claim to be the sole interpreter of the Scriptures is wholly without any divine sanction. So also his exclusive authority to call Church councils is contrary to reason and precedent as evidenced by the fact that several instances from past Church history clearly contradict the claim. He cites a well-known example to disprove the pope's contention: the Council of Nicea was called by Emperor Constantine and not by a pope.

In his *Address to the Christian Nobility* Luther outlined a major programme of reform which should be introduced by the civil power. Citing the authority of the Scriptures Luther reminded the Emperor and the Electors that it was their duty to punish evildoers. The world-wide Christian community fully realized the desperate situation in which the Church of the day lay languishing and how badly it stood in swift need of change and reform. When Luther surveyed the condition of the Catholic Church of his time he could perceive not even the slightest inclination on the part of the leaders of the behemoth, the Catholic Church to cleanse it and restore it to spiritual health and wholeness. It was quite evident from the current malaise in which the Church lingered that either it was unable or unwilling to reform itself from within. Therefore Luther believed that it was incumbent on the civil powers, rather it was their bounden duty to step in and bring about reform in the vital organs of the Church. To begin with, the greatest service that the rulers of Germany can render to their people is to ameliorate the poor economic condition of the common people of Germany by forbidding Rome to make excessive monetary demands on the common people of the land. The opulence in which the pope and his regal court live is there for everyone to see. Their extravagance had already drained Italy of its financial resources. Now it has turned its attention to Germany and threatens to ruin it too. Luther warns the rulers of Germany that unless they restrain the exorbitant levies imposed on Germany by the avarice of Rome, it too will be brought to its knees to the detriment of one and all, of both rulers and the ruled. Luther directs a very timely and pertinent question to the civil authorities: do the Cardinals and their splendid courts serve any purpose other than eating up the wealth of the country? A modest beginning in the right direction would be for the rulers of Germany to order an immediate suspension of the payment of the so called *annates*.[2] Luther is of the view that suspension is insufficient and can only be regarded as an initial step in the right direction and that it should be followed up with the complete abolition of this burdensome levy.

One of the severest censures levelled against Luther in his role as a theological polemist is that, in the heat of passion, he often tended to forget the supreme Christian values of charity, compassion and forgiveness. Though this is not offered in justification of the often crude, combative, and rude tone of some of his exchanges, let us not forget that he was only retorting measure for measure, a Roland for an Oliver, to the injustice and inhumanity meted out to him from his antagonists and adversaries. Moreover, let us

---

[2] Annate: First year's revenue of a see or benefice paid to the pope.

not forget the fact that much of the polemical literature produced by religious controversy during those days was characterized by abusive, violent and vituperative language. The ground reality seems to be that in the heat of argument few can resist the compulsion to be carried away by irrational intolerance and bigotry. It can only be hoped that where unanimity or consensus is impractical or impossible that parties can at least agree to disagree in a sprit of patience, fortitude, and above all, Christian charity. Lamentably what distinguished the entire episode was the absence of the spirit of tolerance and mutual understanding and good will.

It is often suggested that Luther never intended to break away from the Catholic Church and found a Reformation Church and that he merely wanted to cleanse its grosser abuses from within. This is no doubt a legitimate point of view at least as far as the beginning of the struggle for reform is concerned as would have become apparent from the chronicle of its progress. However, it did not call for a prophet's foresight to predict that a contest between an authoritarian and monolithic Medieval Catholic Church on the one hand and an inflexible and inexorable individual's conscience on the other, that it could lead to but one outcome, a total and irrevocable rupture. The foregoing rather detailed narrative must have made it abundantly plain that the chasm between the contending parties was too wide to bridge. No superficial assessment of the reason for the split can adequately account for the deep rift that led to an inevitable division. Even when we exclude from the equation all questions of ego and temperamental incompatibility, we do discern that an irreconcilable divorce was a foregone conclusion from the beginning because the real cause was Luther's new understanding of the Gospel. Subsequent developments, especially in the Roman Church, serve only to confirm the suspicion that owing to the deep gulf that divided Luther's reformation understanding of the Bible and the Catholic Church's traditional stand, the twain were destined never to meet.

The Counter-reformation that began under Pope Paul III (1534-1549) at the Council of Trent (1545-1563), far from seeking any accommodation with the breakaway entity, sounded more like a battle cry against it. Far from showing the least leeway, its doctrinal position tended only to harden further. But the Council did recommend some institutional reforms which were by and large implemented. These include a cessation of the sale of indulgences which in the first place had initiated the crisis within the Church as well as certain steps to correct financial irregularities and abuses on the part of bishops and priests. The religious education of the clergy and the reform of the religious orders also received greater attention. However the attitude of the Roman Catholic Church towards the Protestant denominations turned increasingly hostile and antagonistic, especially after the Council of Trent. To begin with, the Inquisition was instituted in the first instance in Italy to counter the peril to itself from the Lutheran Church. Rome renewed its opposition to any compromise with the Protestant position and rejected all the reforms it espoused. It discounted any reform or change in the basic structure of the medieval Church and reiterated its faith in its doctrines including the sacramental system. It reaffirmed the doctrine of transubstantiation as far as the Mass was concerned. The spiritual value of relics and pilgrimages was also re-emphasized. On the whole despite peripheral improvements and cosmetic changes, the institutional framework of the Catholic Church remained largely unchanged.

However the period coincided with a great religious awakening within the Church. The Jesuit order commissioned by Paul III did yeoman service in spreading the Gospel and in promoting religious and general education. The life and work of the great Christian mystics such as Ignatius of Loyola, Teresa of Avila and later on of John of the Cross produced a great religious awakening, spiritual fervour and zest for holiness among the people. The spiritual exercises outlined by Ignatius Loyola and John of the Cross, piety towards the Virgin, reverence for relics, devoted attention to Christian meditative literature, all these, despite what might be argued against some of these practices, had at least the positive outcome of giving solace and peace of mind to countless Catholics.

Before concluding this part of our study it may be worth our while to inquire what, broadly speaking, is the single most important basic distinction between the Catholic Church and the Protestant and Evangelical Churches. Even at the risk of being accused of providing a rather simplified or even simplistic answer to this serious question, let me try and furnish a functional answer. All shades of Protestantism, whether Lutherans, Baptists, Anabaptists or Presbyterians, generally speaking, anchor their faith and practices on the teaching of Jesus and the Apostles as recorded in the New Testament. The Catholics on the other hand, give almost equal credence to the Bible and the traditions and teaching of the Church. We have a classic example of the importance that the Catholic Church attaches to obedience to its authority in Augustine's peremptory dictum "Roma locuta; causa finita est" (Rome has spoken; the case is concluded). Rome's position has been and still remains largely as it used to be that the dictates of the Church are binding on all Christians.

Finally, what has been the verdict of history on Martin Luther? And what shall be our judgement on him? Was he, in the main, a heretic, a religious fanatic who rent asunder the seamless robe of the Holy, Catholic and Apostolic Roman Church or a man of divine destiny who changed the face of Christendom and the course of history? Laying aside all prepossessions and prejudices, let us try to evaluate dispassionately his lasting legacy and his enduring achievements. As the inaugurator of the Reformation and the initiator of Protestantism, he is one of the defining personalities not only of Church history, but also of the history of human culture and human civilization. His illuminating insights into the Word of God place him beside the great commentators and interpreters of the Bible. As the originator of modern literary German and the illimitable translator of the Bible into German, he will live for ever in the affections of his countrymen. A prolific writer in both Latin and German, his contribution to printing and publishing in the early days of that industry and trade should not be underrated. Luther was principally instrumental in transforming the whole structure of church organization by diminishing the authority of the clergy and at the same time enhancing the role of the laity in its administration and in the divine service. If today the evangelical churches are more liberal than the highly sacerdotal Roman Catholic Church — which sacerdotalism it had inherited from Judaism — is in no small measure owing to the efforts of Luther. Today's many burgeoning evangelical churches in some parts of the world, particularly in North America, owe not a little to the path-breaking work of Luther who made the Gospel the foundation of Christian faith. By making clerical marriage the norm rather than the exception he was instrumental in creating the new institution of the Protestant parsonage. By himself actively participating in composing hymns and making congregational singing an important and integral part of the divine service, Luther looks forward to the great hymn writers of later times such as Charles Wesley, Isaac Watts and Fanny Crosby. Now that in many European countries the Bible was accessible in the local language, family worship and prayer defined the character of the Christian home. His work in popularizing mass education in due course helped to bring about important social and cultural changes. The Reformation probably had many more intangible consequences. How far did the liberal outlook it fostered and promoted assist in releasing vital human energies that flowered into the great awakening which happened in several fields, in political and social changes, in developments in science and industry? Although impossible to measure, its impact might well have been substantial.

Luther has been accused of having been violently anti-Semitic. If he was, and it might well be impossible to exonerate him of the charge, it was a blot he shared with the rest of the Christian world. What was the attitude of the Church towards Jews in those days? Till well into the early years of the nineteenth century in the so-called Christian countries Jews suffered serious disabilities. In England, for instance, they were denied entry into the universities and denied public offices. The country's literature again and again reflects this bias against the Jews whether it is in the Elizabethan play *The Jew of Malta*, or in Shakespeare's *The Merchant of Venice* or Charles Dickens's *Oliver Twist*.[3] No doubt Christian charity should have overcome the all-too-common anti-Jewish prejudice of the times. But it is perhaps too much to demand our post-holocaust liberal attitude from one whose career lay in the first half of the sixteenth century. It is worth remembering in this context that intolerance was not restricted to Jews. Because of his Roman Catholic background, the famous poet Alexander Pope (1688-1744), was deprived of the benefit of a university education, prevented from holding public office and required to live outside a ten-mile radius of London by the anti-Catholic regulations of the time! Prejudice was widespread and was not confined to any one segment of society. In Roman Catholic countries Christians of a Protestant or an evangelical persuasion were ruthlessly hunted down and exterminated.

---

[3] Christopher Marlowe's (1564-1593) play *The Jew of Malta* (1589) provides us with a vivid representation of the intense antipathy with which Christians perceived their Jewish brethren. When the ruler of Turkey demanded tribute from Malta, the governor of the island ordered its Jewish inhabitants to pay it. The wealthy Jew Barabas who resisted, had all his properties confiscated. In retaliation for the gross injustice he indulges in an orgy of violence. Even William Shakespeare with his broad humanity and universal sympathy could not shake off the popular anti-Jewish prejudice in the depiction of Shylock. So also Dickens's Fagin, who keeps an academy for training pickpockets, had to be cast a Jew to make the character credible and acceptable to the public.

A man of many parts and great versatility, a fierce disputant, a distinguished preacher and lecturer, theological controversialist, religious polemist, often combative, at times irascible, Martin Luther is one of those rare human phenomena in history. Of indefatigable resolve and immense nervous energy as publicist and propagandist of Reformation ideas and ideals he has few equals. A man of unshakeable convictions and firm faith, he is worthy to stand beside the Bible's illustrious heroes of faith. It has been remarked that the disciples of Jesus turned the world of the first century upside down. It is no exaggeration to state that this redoubtable champion of liberty of conscience Martin Luther also in some considerable measure changed the world of his time. Undoubtedly he is one of the defining personalities of Church history and indeed of world history.

Chapter 7

THE ENGLISH REFORMATION

> The Bishop of Rome hath no jurisdiction in this Realm of England.
>
> - *Book of Common Prayer*

Unlike the reform movement in Europe that started as a movement for the correction of financial and other abuses within the Catholic Church and gradually moved on from there to the reform of doctrinal errors, Reformation in England had a curious, rather bizarre beginning. If German nationalism versus Italian hegemony was a contributory cause that entered the reform movement at a subsequent stage, in England it was almost wholly part of state policy. King Henry VIII who was its prime protagonist was in fact a doughty champion of Church supremacy and papal privileges and prerogatives. When the initial rumblings of Luther's critique of certain practices within the Catholic Church reached the island, both Church and state stood solidly behind Rome. For instance, in 1521, when support for the reform movement was gaining ground in Germany, John Fisher, bishop of Rochester (1459-1535) preached a widely-welcomed sermon against Luther. His defence of the pope on theological grounds earned him wide recognition in Europe. Not to be behind hand, for his part, Henry wrote a highly acclaimed pamphlet titled *Assertio Septem Sacramentorum Adversus Martinum Lutherum* (1521) defending the seven sacraments of the Catholic Church against Luther's attack. A highly gratified Pope Clement VII (Guilio de Medici) honoured the monarch with the ecclesiastical title *Fidei Defensor* (Defender of the Faith). Moreover in 1531 Henry ordered the public burning of Luther's books to demonstrate his opposition to the Reformation and his allegiance to Rome.

The rupture with Rome occurred, not over doctrinal differences with the Catholic Church, but for reasons which were partly personal and partly political, but wholly earthy, although in the process it brought about reform in the faith and practice of the Anglican Church.

England's young king was a highly accomplished man. Graceful and handsome, he was a scholar, a musician, a patron of the arts and of learning. However, there was a streak of cruelty and ruthlessness in his personality which was in frequent evidence in his later years. In order to see the unfolding events in their true perspective, we need now to take a look not only at the history of the country at the time, but also peep into Henry's domestic situation. Being the younger—really the second—son of the Tudor monarch Henry VII, the future Henry VIII was not groomed for kingship. Arthur, his older brother was the king-in-waiting. The politically astute Henry Tudor concluded a marriage for Arthur with Catherine of Aragon, the daughter of Ferdinand of Aragon and Isabella of Castile.[1] The early demise of Arthur made the second son Henry the heir-apparent. In order to cement relations between Spain and England, Henry was induced to marry Arthur's widow although the canon law forbade such a union. To legitimize the union a special dispensation from Pope Julius II was procured, but on the factitious reasoning of non-consummation of the nuptials. After a certain period of married bliss Henry distanced himself more and more from Catherine. Apparently many were the reasons. They had a daughter, Mary, the future 'bloody Mary' of the history books, but Catherine failed to produce a male heir to Henry and a male heir the king desperately wished to have for the continuance of the Tudor dynasty. Henry's roving amorous eyes grew fascinated with a certain Anne Boleyn, a lady-in-

---

[1] Ferdinand of Aragon (1452-1516) married Isabella of Castile (1451-1504) in 1469, thereby creating a powerful Spain by uniting the kingdoms of Aragon and Castile. Isabella was known as *la Catolica* (the Catholic).

waiting on the queen, while Catherine was growing ever more portly and plain by the day. As a Christian man and a Catholic king, he was spiritually also perturbed because Leviticus expressly forbade his union with his brother's widow. Was the denial of a male heir divine punishment for his sin? The thought seems to have been gnawing at his heart. The king saw the remedy for this dire situation in divorcing Catherine and marrying Anne who showed all signs of being capable of giving Henry the male heir he craved. The pope was again approached, this time by England alone, to declare Henry's marriage to Catherine null and void as it contravened canon law. This time the pope could not oblige England because Spain opposed the move and the pope was at that juncture a virtual prisoner of Spain as Spanish troops had entered Rome and ransacked the city. Moreover Catherine's nephew Charles V[2] was now the Holy Roman Emperor! Pugnacious by nature and proud of his skill as a pugilist, pope or no pope, Henry must have his way. This is the background of how the English Reformation came about.

In the breach with Rome what stands out in the popular psyche is the abrogation of the power of the pope and the Curia and the assumption by the reigning monarch of the sovereignty of the English Church. By invoking the divine right of kings, Henry assumed the title the supreme governor of the Church. This was done in the years 1533-34 by a series of acts of king-in-parliament. These epoch-making changes happened hot on the heels of Luther launching his tirade against Rome and a century and a half after Wycliffe's heroic battle against the corrupt medieval Church. The changes effected through the king's reforms were more far-reaching than at first might appear. The declaration of the independence of the national Church from Rome effectively

---

[2] Charles V was the grandson of Ferdinand of Aragon and Isabella of Castile through his mother Joanna (the mad). Joanna was the daughter of Ferdinand and Isabella.

brought the all-powerful clergy under the control of the laity. The dissolution of the monasteries that quickly followed the Act of Supremacy brought about unparalleled social and economic changes in the country. Within the next few years much of the Church's wealth in the form of real estate, and with it much of the power and influence it represented, passed into the hands of a new class of landed gentry. The triumph of the king was the culmination of a tussle between Rome and Westminster which began in the fourteenth-century against the interference of the pope and the Curia in the appointment of English bishops and the assignment of the Church's benefices to the clergy. In this Henry was strongly supported by an emerging middle class instructed in religious matters through their reading of the vernacular printed Bible and polemical literature relating to the reform movement brought into the island from Western Europe. Within a few years many of the vestiges of medieval Catholicism which the new enlightened middle classes regarded as mere superstition disappeared from the Anglican Church. These included Communion without adherence to the belief in transubstantiation of the Catholic Mass, congregational worship in song and prayer, a married clergy and the adoption of the sole authority of the Bible for Christian faith and doctrine. The religious life of the people was no longer confined to the church premises. With the permission to marry extended to the clergy during the reign of the boy king Edward VI, the married state was exalted above the medieval monastic ideal of celibacy and isolation from society. In addition to church worship, family worship with hymn singing, Bible reading, and prayer became the model of the Christian family.

England may be said to have shed most of the trappings of medievalism and emerged into the light of modernity with King Henry unleashing an anti-clerical revolution that had been simmering for almost two centuries past. However, despite his anti-clericalism, the reform that Henry envisaged and tried to carry out was in many ways really orthodox and Catholic. It was true that he was set firmly against Rome. But he was equally against all forms of new-fangled Protestant and Reformation notions. The influence of the Humanists, Erasmus, More and others may have helped to turn the tide of society against monks, friars and the like who were detested as social parasites and religious obscurants. The pent-up dislike of the monks and friars was used by Henry in dissolving these orders and appropriating their properties. As in Germany, the English Reformation was a triumph for nationalism over Italian hegemony masquerading as internationalism and universalism. Purging the worship of some of its arcane ritualism and getting rid of some of the corrupt practices within the Church's administration and religious orders were no doubt positive gains. However, it was not all gain. The movement was accompanied by great losses too.

Children's education was one of the first casualties of the depredations of the religious houses. In the darkest phases of European history it was the great monasteries and abbeys which had kept the light of knowledge burning. For centuries past the Church, and not so much the state, had been the great civilizing force in society so much so that the noted art historian Kenneth Clark makes bold to assert that Western civilization is largely a creation of the Church.[3] Even the earliest universities of Europe such as Paris, Oxford and Cambridge grew out of ecclesiastical institutions. The University of Paris, for instance, was an outgrowth of Notre Dame Cathedral. Confining ourselves to the situation in England, many of the schools had been founded and fostered by monasteries and abbeys. Even nunneries played no insignificant role in the training of young women, as what small provision for a girl child's education existed in the country had been supplied by them. Apart from imparting education to children these religious foundations had been

---

[3] Kenneth Clark, *Civilization* (New York: Harper & Row), 1969.

great repositories of books. The savage vandalism of libraries and the destruction of enormous quantities of books that accompanied the depredations was an irreparable loss to learning. With the sudden disappearance of these institutions education in the country suffered a serious setback. Soon after the English Reformation enrolment at Oxford and Cambridge saw a steep fall. Despite the gains achieved by the Reformation by purging the Church of many apparently meaningless superstitions and rituals, the losses suffered in fields such as education left a deep void. It took decades to fill the void by fresh foundations.

The reform initiated by Henry may have left unaffected the fundamentals of the Catholic faith. But in the ensuing years many more changes were effected in matters of faith and doctrine as we shall presently see. At a Convocation of the archbishops and bishops of the realm held in London in 1562, the thirty-nine "Articles of Religion" were approved. Their ostensible purpose was the avoidance of diversity of opinions and the working out of a consensus. These set out in great detail the doctrines which should guide the Church of England. An examination of the Articles shows how far-reaching many of the reforms were, although the cardinal creeds of the Church remained unaltered and only reaffirmed. Many of the proposed changes took the reform movement much farther than originally envisaged by Henry VIII. On a careful examination they will be seen as in greater consonance with the Reformation affirmations of Luther. The cornerstone of the Reformation credo that we are justified by faith and not through meritorious works receives reiterated emphasis in Articles XI and XII. The belief in purgatory, pardons, the worship of images and relics was abrogated as it enjoyed no Biblical sanction and as it was repugnant to the Word of God. So also transubstantiation was dismissed as a superstition in that it was not authorised by Holy Writ. Nevertheless, the Articles of Religion clearly laid down that the Communion, when partaken in faith, was a much deeper and more meaningful experience than a mere memorial of Christ's sacrifice. Here is what Article XXVIII "Of the Lord's Supper" affirms. "The Supper of the Lord is not only a sign of the love that Christians ought to have among themselves one to another: but rather is a Sacrament of our Redemption by Christ's death: insomuch that to such as rightly, worthily, and with faith, receive the same, the Bread which we break is a partaking of the Body of Christ; and likewise the Cup of Blessing is a partaking of the Blood of Christ." Communion in both kinds, a key demand of the reformers on the Continent, was restored by the Anglican Church also as evidenced by Article XXX which clearly laid it down that laymen ought not to be denied the Cup of the Lord. It spelt out in plain language that both parts of the sacrament should be administered to all Christians alike. Again in agreement with Luther's teaching, the Anglican Church recognized only the sacraments of baptism and Holy Communion. The remaining five of the Roman Church were not ordained by Christ and therefore were no longer regarded as sacraments by the Church of England. Ministers were once again declared free to marry like other Christians because Scripture did not forbid them to do so. On the whole, while many things changed, many continued without alteration. The chief endeavour seems to have been to avoid extremes and to curb excessive zeal and unbridled enthusiasm of some extreme Protestant sects and to keep clear of gross departures from Scripture which had crept into the Roman Church over the centuries. The most distinguishing feature in the ethos of the Anglican Church continues to be its genius for keeping to the via media.

Chapter 8

THE AFTERMATH: CALVINISTS, PURITANS AND DISSIDENTS

In our survey of the aftermath of the Reformation we propose to deal with Calvinism, Puritanism, and the remaining sects under the broad heading of Dissidence. We shall focus on the life and work of three of the principal protagonists of these movements, namely John Calvin, Huldreich Zwingli and John Knox. We shall speak of Calvin in some detail and depth as Calvinism was destined to exert the most profound impact on the future fortunes of Christianity, especially after its transplantation on the North American continent.

It was inevitable that once the new Lutheran theology and church re-organization had permeated Germany, they should extend their influence into the neighbouring regions. And what more fertile soil could be desired for their transplantation than the freer nations of Switzerland and the Netherlands? Of all the countries of Europe Switzerland was the readiest to receive the seeds of the renewal of the Christian faith as it was one of the freest countries of Europe, being made up of thirteen self-governing city-states called cantons. The work of Zwingli and Calvin was concentrated in two of these self-governing city-states, namely Zurich and Geneva respectively, but it touched almost the entire country and was destined to impact Christian communities in many parts of the world. Despite Calvin's deeper and more long-lasting impact, Zwingli calls for earlier treatment as his work preceded that of Calvin.

Although an imitator and follower of Luther in many respects, Zwingli differed in quite significant ways from the German reformer. Though well versed in philosophy and theology in the scholastic tradition of medieval Christianity, Luther's temperament had a mystical and pietistic bent. Zwingli, on the other hand, inclined more to the humanistic tradition owing to his intellectual and critical frame of mind. As a consequence, despite the identity of their views on many matters of doctrine and faith, Zwingli, it would seem, had arrived at his position through an independent study of the Bible. That the mystical strain in Luther's character was the direct antithesis of the more rational outlook of Zwingli is best exemplified in their differing attitudes to the Holy Communion. While both deemed the Roman Catholic doctrine of transubstantiation erroneous, for Luther the Lord's Supper was much more than a memorial to a poignant historical event. Luther clung to the faith that, as far as the believer was concerned, Christ was spiritually present in the elements of the Communion. The more critical and rational mind of Zwingli scoffed at the notion. He interpreted the exhortation of Jesus to remember his sacrifice at each and every communal love fest quite literally and was not prepared to concede any further ground to Luther's sensitivity to the subject.

The Swiss-born Zwingli (1484-1531) attended the university both at Vienna and Basel where he became attracted to the New Learning that had broken out all over Europe. He fell under the spell of Erasmus, studied his Greek New Testament and became an ardent advocate of Church reform. However, it is interesting to note that his beginnings were in the Catholic Church. Operating out of Zurich, in 1518 he obtained the powerful office of 'People's Priest' at its cathedral. There he became immensely popular for his opposition to Swiss mercenaries serving in foreign lands. Pretty soon he became a convert to the new Protestant theology that was radiating through several parts of Europe. Like Luther, he was fiercely opposed to the sale of indulgences by the Catholic Church. By 1523 Zurich had fully adopted Zwingli's ecclesiastical reforms and became the first Protestant state outside of Germany. It was only a matter of time before it spread to the remaining city-states within Switzerland.

Zwingli's theology is simplicity itself. Being wholly scripture-oriented, it was rooted in the single principle that what the Bible taught was mandatory and called for implicit obedience by each and every Christian. Its corollary was equally valid: whatever was not in the Bible had no place in Christian theology. The practical application of this principle meant that for Zwingli religion meant the spiritual transformation of the individual human being as a result of his personal transaction with God. It called for a purification and diminution of Church ritual and ceremony and emphasized a more direct relationship between man and his maker with little or no mediation from outside agents. Gradually he succeeded in bringing the Zurich city council to his innovative ideas. Thus in lieu of the Catholic Mass the Zurich churches observed the Holy Communion. Church services were made simpler with little or no ritual or ceremony. Like Luther, Zwingli held to the belief that faith alone was requisite for one's salvation. But unlike Luther, and more akin to the views later propounded by Calvin, Zwingli held a rather exclusive view of the Church that it was a body of believers predestined by God for salvation due to no merit of its own, but wholly dependent on the sheer choice of God. From his strong base in Zurich, Zwingli hoped to advance the cause of Protestantism throughout Switzerland. But this was not to be. In the religious wars that ensued he lost his life in 1531, leaving it to Calvin to complete that task.

If Zwingli established in Zurich a church that was wholly Scripture-centred, the credit for having taken the principle of Biblical orientation to its extreme logical conclusion and extending the principle not only to individual and collective religious life but also to social organization and even to political structures and governments legitimately belongs to Calvin (1509-1564). Calvin's ideas and his brand of theology were to have deeper and wider influence on Western thought than those of Zwingli. The legacy of the Puritan brand of Calvinism is perceptible in much of Western thought even today and forms an integral part of American culture. Born in 1509 to a notary in Noyon, Picardy, John Calvin attended the University of Paris. After securing a master's degree in arts, to fulfil his father's aspiration to train him for the practice of the law, he enrolled as a law student at the University of Orleans. Meanwhile he studied Greek and Hebrew at the College de France in Paris and absorbed himself in humanistic studies. His intense and sustained interest in the classical authors bore fruit in his first publication, a commentary on Seneca. However, despite the versatility of his interests, the central passion and preoccupation of his life all along had been and continued to be, religion. Unlike Luther whose discovery of the Bible happened after he had scoured the fields of medieval Christianity and scholastic philosophy, Calvin headed straight to the Bible, the exposition of Christian doctrine in Paul's epistles, and the commentaries of Augustine of Hippo. Some time during 1533-34 he went through a profound religious conversion. He became convinced of the total depravity of man and the absolute holiness, justice and sovereignty of God. From that time onwards he felt that he was an agent and an instrument in the hands of God, chosen by Him to spread the truth. He lived out the rest of his life committed to carry out that charge.

To escape the persecution of Protestants and Humanists begun by King Francis I of France, Calvin sought refuge in Basel, a citadel of the Reformation movement. In this enlightened city in 1536 his magnum opus the *Institutes of the Christian Religion* was published. In the course of a career marked by strange vicissitudes, in June of the same year Calvin chanced to stop at Geneva for a night's rest. But providence had decreed otherwise as it had long-range plans for him in the city. Barring brief absences, he was destined by God, as he came to accept it, to spend the rest of his life there; he died in 1564. Unlike the free city states of Zurich, Bern, Basel and others which had converted to Protestantism early, Geneva which had been ruled by the House of Savoy, an Italian princely family had been late in embracing ideas of the Reformation. Being a border town in close proximity to France, it had the double disadvantage of being mainly French speaking, whereas the Protestant cantons were mainly German speaking and so more amenable to the influence of the Lutheran Reformation. However, finally the citizens of Geneva broke free from their tutelage to Savoy and reformers from the canton of Bern converted the city to Protestantism by 1535. It was at this critical juncture that Calvin chanced to arrive in the city. The citizens of Geneva prevailed upon him to remain in the city and build an evangelical and reformed church there. As a result of his work in Geneva he radically changed the face of Protestant Christianity. Calvin devoted the rest of his life to organizing Geneva into a theocratic city-state. Modelling itself on the apostolic church of the first century, the reformed church comprised four orders of officials: pastors, teachers, elders and deacons. The main task set before a pastor — also called a minister — was to preach the word of God. He was in charge of administering the sacraments too. The exercise of disciplinary duty over erring members of the congregation also formed part of his responsibilities. Pastors were required to receive the assent of the general assembly of the church and needed the consent of the city council for confirmation in the office. Instruction on doctrine, faith and discipline was the special province of the teachers, technically styled doctors after the Jewish scribes or doctors of the law. In Calvin's scheme of things education played a prominent part and church schools received his special and personal care. The elders were lay leaders who formed the central matrix of the ecclesiastical establishment. As in the apostolic church, the deacons looked after the distribution of charity to the poor and needy.

Calvin's claim to fame as a theologian rests on his magnum opus, the *Institutes* which comprises a masterly and scholarly synthesis of Protestant thought. The main thesis of the book is grounded upon a literal interpretation of the story of Creation in Genesis. It asserts that the depravity of human nature is consequent on the Fall of Man. It further states that due to the omnipotence and omniscience of the Almighty, His true nature man can in no manner compass. Yet the Word of God illumines his mind sufficiently for him to acknowledge the sovereignty of God and the creature's duty for abject subjection to the will of the Creator. The irrefutable law of God is encrypted in the Bible and human conduct should be governed by its dictates and there can be absolutely no dilution of its standards. Five articles of faith are generally cited as constituting the foundation stone of Calvinist theology. First of all, consequent on the Fall of Adam, his progeny is totally depraved and unable to work out its salvation. The Bible categorically endorses the total depravity of man and Calvin's stand on the matter has full Biblical support. Next, Calvinism holds that election and reprobation are wholly dependent on God's will and that human merit and good works are irrelevant as far as God's choice is concerned. In other words, irrespective of what we do or fail to do, we are all predestined either for election or reprobation. Thirdly, salvation is achieved solely through the loving self-immolation of Jesus Christ. Fourthly, the grace of God is gratuitously bestowed upon man and can never be earned through meritorious works. The last article of Calvinist faith is usually called the perseverance of the saints. It implies that the elect of God are granted divine power to do His will. At times it is referred to as the theory of the 'living saints'. Unlike the Roman Catholic Church which canonizes certain individuals, Calvinists visualize the Church as a body of living saints.

We do not have to go far to find Biblical support for the doctrine of man's moral depravity. What do these words of

St. Paul signify except the total depravity of unregenerate natural man?

> I do not understand my behaviour, for I am not doing what I want to, but the very things I hate. And if I do what I don't want to do, it is evident that I agree that God's Law is good. So I am not really the one doing the wrong—it is sin living within me that does it. For I know that there is nothing good in me, that is, in my sinful nature. The desire to do right is there, but not the power to do it. For I do not do the good that I really want to do, but instead I do the evil that I don't want to do.[1]

In the popular psyche Calvinism is inextricably intertwined with the dogma of predestination, an inescapable concomitant of God's attribute of omniscience. In over four chapters of the *Institutes*, its author buttresses the doctrine of predestination by marshalling a whole host of corroborative evidence, all cited from the Bible. In spite of the massive evidence marshalled by Calvin to buttress his central thesis, predestination poses several conundrums. If God's omniscience supports the doctrine that human beings are predestined either for salvation or reprobation, His omnipotence seems to militate against it. And how does one reconcile the categorical affirmation of Jesus in the context of the episode of the rich young man (Matthew 19: 16-30; Mark 10: 17-31; Luke 18: 18-30) that "all things are possible with God" and Jesus' parable of the unjust judge with the Calvinist dogma of reprobation or their doctrinaire approach to it? If an unjust human agent could be made to show mercy to a litigant on her continual importunity (Luke 18: 1-8), wouldn't a loving God be merciful to a repentant sinner on his fervent prayers and petitions? After all, isn't the All-Knowing One equally the All-Loving One too?[2]

The stern and severe outlook of Calvin on discipline and morality reminds me of the opening lines of William Wordsworth's "Ode to Duty."

---

[1] Romans 7: 15-19 (The New Translation).
[2] Compare: The very God! Think, Abib; dost thou think?
So, the All-Great, were the All-Loving too. . .
From "Karshish" (a poem by Robert Browning).

> Stern Daughter of the Voice of God
> O Duty! If that name thou love
> Who art a light to guide, a rod
> To check the erring, and reprove;
> Thou, who art victory and law
> When empty terrors overawe;
> From vain temptations dost set free;
> And calmest the weary strife of frail humanity!

In the holy commonwealth that Calvin established in Geneva, he enforced a rigorous and ruthless Christian code of conduct. But when all is said and done, with the Calvinistic Church, argus-eyed, holding surveillance over our conscience, aren't we in peril of lapsing into the rigorous regimen of Pharisaism and the unavoidable hypocrisy that goes along with it? Be that as it may, the full flowering of Calvinism was displayed in the Presbyterianism of Scotland and the Puritanism of American New England.

The seeds of Puritanism on the eastern shores of North America were sowed by a handful of religious refugees from England. It was in 1609 that a group of extreme religious radicals called Brownists or Separatists—they had separated themselves from the established Anglican Church—set sail for Holland.[3] First they went to Amsterdam and from there moved to Leyden. Looking for a more favourable environment to establish their Christian commonwealth, they set sail in the *Mayflower* for the New World and arrived at Cape Cod in November 1620. Thus it was that through the agency of the Pilgrim Fathers that a pure form of Puritanism reached the eastern shores of New England in North America. Still this pioneer community constituted but a trickle which was followed in the coming decades with massive migrations from England, Scotland and parts of Europe.

---

[3] In his *A Treatise of Reformation* (1582), its author Robert Browne argued that those who were genuine followers of Jesus Christ and His Gospel ought to separate themselves from the Anglican Church—which he thought consisted largely of nominal Christians—and worship separately. This community that separated themselves came to be known as Separatists or Brownists.

Protestant sects such as the Congregationalists, Presbyterians, Methodists, Baptists, Unitarians, Quakers, and the like that we find in the United States today are all offshoots of these early Puritans and Presbyterians from England and Scotland. Puritan ways of thought and action—what might be loosely termed the Puritan ethic—have had the most profound impact on the course of the history and culture of the United States. However it is good to bear in mind that although the rather narrow Puritan and the more broadly liberal Protestant thinking dominate the American religious and cultural landscape even to this day, several other streams flowing from different sources have mingled in its waters.

The Scottish Reformation

The Scottish Reformation that gave birth to the Presbyterian Church there was principally due to the life-work of John Knox. Educated at the University of St. Andrews, John Knox (1510-1572), after a troubled early career, went to England where he served as chaplain to England's boy-king Edward VI. While living in London he probably played a role in reforming *A Book of Common Prayer*, commonly called the *Prayer Book*. During his sojourn in England and later in exile on the Continent, there poured out from his pen numerous pamphlets, all either exposing the deficiencies and defects of the Catholic Church or supporting the agenda of the religious reformers. Because of his zeal for the reformist cause, during the regime of the Roman Catholic Mary Tudor, he was forced to flee the island and seek refuge in Geneva where he met John Calvin. He wholeheartedly endorsed—and himself imbibed—most of the tenets of Calvinism including Calvin's uncompromising attachment to the dogma of predestination. Therefore John Calvin may be said to be Knox's spiritual mentor. On leaving Geneva he moved to Frankfurt-on-the-Main where he took up the leadership of the English Refugee Church there. However, his extreme Puritanical views caused a rift in the congregation which compelled him to relinquish the charge and return to Geneva.

In the nonage of Mary Queen of Scots—she was queen before she was a week old—her mother Mary of Guise (also known as Mary of Lorraine) acted as Regent of Scotland. The attempt of the Regent to root out Protestantism from Scotland evoked a series of epistles and pamphlets from Knox arraigning her policies and exhorting the faithful to endure affliction and assuring them of future times of refreshment. During the pro-Roman regimes of the two Marys in England and Scotland and while languishing abroad as a fugitive, Knox bitterly bewailed his lot and passionately longed to preach Protestantism in the island. With the triumph of the reforming party in Scotland, Knox was enabled in 1559 to return to his native land. He now turned his attention to the twin interests of his life, namely, religion and education. His ambition to found a school in every parish and a feeder school in every town from where the ablest pupils would be despatched to the country's three universities could not be fully fulfilled in his lifetime owing chiefly to the poverty of the people. Nevertheless, his efforts achieved considerable success in making Scotland's educational system the pride and boast of the people. Eventually Knox's ideal bore fruit in nurturing a vigorous intellectual ethos in the country. His magnum opus and the chief literary monument to the Scottish Reformation is *The History of the Reformation in Scotland*. The title is rather misleading as the work is more in the nature of an apologia for the displacement of Scotland's ancient religion with the new Presbyterian form of faith. It is not really an out and out historical narrative. Knox's account of his interviews with Mary Queen of Scots constitutes the most interesting part of the work.

A man of profound convictions, the singular aim of Knox's life was to secure the success of the Scottish Reformation. Indeed, his entire life work was devoted to the fulfilment of that goal. The fittest tool for implementing the goal, he was convinced, was the spread of literacy and education. In the role he played as a propagandist for education he is the counterpart of Philip Melanchthon who played an analogous role in Germany. A religious belief solely based on the Bible and a sound system of national education was the foundation of the Christian Commonwealth that he envisaged. The passionate convictions and the towering personality of John Knox dominate the Scottish Presbyterian landscape. A doughty defender of the dogma of predestination, he wrote a lengthy volume on it. Yet it must yield pride of place to Calvin's *Institutes* which will maintain its pre-eminent position as the bible of predestination. As we hinted in connection with Calvinism, a vein of self-righteousness is the besetting sin of those who imagine that they are the elect of God. For, after all, isn't all human righteousness a misnomer for self-righteousness, which in its turn a euphemism for the sin of pride? The hypocrisy that envelops the Puritan's pride in his goodness is held up to ridicule in "Holy Willy's Prayer" by Robert Burns.[4] The poem should be read in its entirety to enjoy the full force of its satire. Here is a short sample that exposes the speaker's egotism and self-righteousness.

> Yet I am here, a chosen sample,
> To show thy grace is great and ample:
> I'm here, a pillar o' thy temple
> Strong as a rock,
> A guide, a ruler and example
> To all thy flock.

Now it remains for us to look briefly at, under the broad heading of Christian Dissidents, an amorphous group who for conscience's sake were either unable or unwilling to conform to the faith and practice of the Established Anglican

---

[4] Scotland's national poet Robert Burns (1759-1796) attacks the Calvinist doctrine of predestination in the poem. William Fisher, the speaker of the poem is an elder of his parish. A strict Calvinist, Fisher is convinced that he is predestined to salvation by the grace of God. The poem progressively reveals the speaker's appalling egotism and self-complacency which are disguised as humility. The hidden side of election and predestination is shown for what it is, obnoxious egotism, vanity and pharisaism.

Church. Religious dissent, like other forms of social dissent, has a long history. It is much anterior to the Reformation and pre-dates it by decades and even generations. We may begin this section with the followers and the bare-foot priests of John Wycliffe. Who are the Dissidents known as the Lollards? The Shorter Oxford English Dictionary (SOED) defines Lollard as "a name of contempt given in the fourteenth century to certain heretics, who were either followers of Wycliffe or held opinions similar to his". In the eyes of the ecclesiastical establishment, the Lollards — successors to dissident Christian groups from the fourteenth-century onwards — were a socially disruptive group hostile to many of the traditional practices of the Catholic Church. They were antipathetic to the Catholic Mass with its emphasis on transubstantiation. They disapproved of the need to confess their sins to the clergy. They were also against fasting, going on pilgrimages and praying before the images of the saints. Above all, they wanted to have direct access to the Bible in the vernacular.

Unlike the Lollards who were a native phenomenon, Baptists and Anabaptists[5] who appeared in England in the first half of the sixteenth-century, received their stimulus and inspiration from across the Channel. While they share many features of their faith with other Puritan and evangelical groups such as the Calvinists, their distinctive stamp continues to be their insistence on the adult baptism of the born-again Christian. Most of their fellow-Christians consider this insistence a rather scandalous thing because infant christening had been and continues to be the usual custom among most Christian churches for centuries. Their theology is grounded in a literal interpretation of the Bible. They pin their faith on the basic conviction that all Scripture is inspired by God. They wholeheartedly subscribe to Paul's statement that "all

---

[5] The original Greek term for 'to baptize' meant 'to immerse'. The word Anabaptist means to re-baptize. Anabaptists deny the validity of infant baptism and insist on re-baptizing those who had received infant baptism.

THE AFTERMATH: CALVINISTS, PURITANS AND DISSIDENTS 113

scripture is given by inspiration of God, and is profitable for doctrine, for reproof, for correction, for instruction in righteousness that the man of God may be perfect, thoroughly furnished unto all good works" (II Timothy 3:16-17). Their theology is thus solely and wholly Bible-centred. Both groups strive to restore the purity and simplicity of apostolic Christianity in their communities. They wish to emulate the values that Jesus propounded in the Sermon on the Mount as their code of moral conduct and try hard to make it literally binding upon each and every twice-born Christian. As a natural corollary, they eschew violence in any form and in all circumstances, abhor oaths, private possessions, bodily adornment, revelling and drunkenness. In the beginning there were two main groups: General Baptists and Particular Baptists. While General Baptists believe that salvation is open to all believers Particular Baptists would restrict it to the 'elect'. In the early days governments looked at them as a subversive group as they refused to take part in the defence of the country.

In this broad survey we have dealt only with the major divisions and personalities and have had to exclude from it numerous non-conformist and dissident groups which have appeared and disappeared from time to time. Our focus having been on Luther and the Reformation, only a cursory survey of subsidiary themes has been attempted.

Chapter 9

CONCLUSION

While dealing with the Apostolic Church I ventured the statement that the principal protagonist in the "Young Church in Action" was not one of the Apostles, not a human agent at all, but the Holy Spirit. I do believe that, even though the Reformation may have started with a rather innocuous theological debate proposed by Martin Luther, the catalyst that propelled it into a pan-European movement and the dynamic that brought it to fruition was none other than the Spirit of God, the Lord of all history. When all is said and done, in the final analysis, has the Reformation initiated by Luther, Calvin, Zwingli, Knox and others and the birth of the various Protestant and other reformed churches, purged the Church of heresies, schisms, doctrinal errors, corruption in Church administration and among the clergy? Like the poor, corrupt practices are likely to linger among us for all time to come. It is an ancient problem, and it is very much an issue today and it is likely to continue to challenge us in the future also. Isn't Church reformation, indeed, a re-formation of the Church, still a live process that is and ought to be always a work in progress? Humanity being a conglomeration of sinners, the visible Church is bound to be an imperfect institution. Here is the prophet Ezekiel railing against contemporary Jewish priests for neglecting their flock.

> And the word of the Lord came unto me, saying, Son of man, prophesy against the shepherds of Israel, prophesy, and say unto them, Thus saith the Lord God unto the shepherds; Woe be to the shepherds of Israel that do feed themselves! Should not the shepherds feed the flocks? Ye eat the fat, and ye clothe you with the wool, ye kill them that are fed: but ye feed not the flock. The diseased have ye not strengthened, neither have ye healed that which was sick, neither have ye bound up that which was broken, neither have ye brought again that which was driven away, neither have ye sought

that which was lost; but with force and with cruelty have ye ruled them. And they were scattered because there is no shepherd: and they became meat to all the beasts of the field, when they were scattered. My sheep wandered through all the mountains, and upon every high hill; yea, my flock was scattered upon all the face of the earth, and none did search or seek after them. Therefore, ye shepherds, hear the word of the Lord; As I live, saith the Lord God, surely because my flock became a prey, and my flock became meat to every beast of the field, because there was no shepherd, neither did my shepherds search for my flock, but the shepherds fed themselves, and fed not my flock; Therefore, O ye shepherds, hear the word of the Lord; Thus saith the Lord God; Behold, I am against the shepherds; and I will require my flock at their hand, and cause them to cease from feeding the flock; neither shall the shepherds feed themselves any more; for I will deliver my flock from their mouth, that they may not be meat for them (Ezekiel 34: 1-10).

The New Testament Epistles reveal that even in the first century self-seeking teachers were actively propagating heresies and false doctrines. Bent only on filling their belly by making the ministry the means of earning an easy and comfortable livelihood, they were already posing a danger to the dissemination of the true Gospel.

For there are certain men crept in unawares, who were before of old ordained to this condemnation, ungodly men, turning the grace of our God into lasciviousness, and denying the only Lord God, and our Lord Jesus Christ. . . . These are spots in your feasts of charity, when they feast with you, feeding themselves without fear. (Jude, verses 4, 12).

More than a century after Luther we find the English poet John Milton castigating the Anglican clergy of his time. The poet's indignation is directed more at the Roman Catholic Church which is portrayed as "grim wolf with privy paw" in the extract from the poem given below. Divine vengeance against both is depicted as a "two-handed engine" that will destroy both the erring Churches. In this elegy written to lament the death by drowning of Edward King, his fellow-student at Christ College, Cambridge, and musing on the circumstance that had he lived he may have been an exemplary Christian minister, the Puritan spirit in Milton extrapolates the situation to launch a tirade against the self-serving clergymen of his time. Modelled on classical Greek elegies, the rear of the cavalcade of mourners is brought up by Simon Peter who holds the keys of the Kingdom. It is he who impersonates the poet.

> Last came and last did go,
> The Pilot of the Galilean lake;
> Two massy keys he bore of metals twain
> (The golden opes, the iron shuts amain).
> He shook his mitred locks, and stern bespake:
> 'How well could I have spared for thee, young swain,
> Enow of such as for their bellies' sake,
> Creep and intrude, and climb into the fold!
> Of other care they little reckoning make
> Than how to scramble at the shearers' feast,
> And shove away the worthy bidden guest.
> Blind mouths! That scarce themselves know how to hold
> A sheep-hook, or have learnt aught else the least
> That to the faithful herdsman's art belongs!
> What recks it them? What need they? They are sped;
> And when they list, their lean and flashy songs
> Grate on their scrannel pipes of wretched straw;
> The hungry sheep look up, and are not fed,
> But swollen with wind, and the rank mist they draw,
> Rot inwardly, and foul contagion spread;
> Beside what the grim wolf with privy paw
> Daily devours apace, and nothing said;
> But that two-handed engine at the door
> Stands ready to smite once, and smite no more' (*Lycidas*, ll.108-121).

Not content with the English Reformation, we find John and Charles Wesley trying to reform the Anglican Church of their day only to find them being put out of the Anglican Communion and having to establish a new foundation, the Methodist Church. It would appear that imperfection is the stamp of all human institutions. Only a Church fully directed by the Holy Spirit can be the truly Holy, Catholic and Apostolic Church. There is little prospect of that till Kingdom Come. "On the earth the broken arcs; in the heaven, a perfect round."[1] But inevitably the Church, the bride of the Lamb

---

[1] Robert Browning, "Abt Vogler," l. 72.

will have made herself fully ready by the time of the wedding supper of the Lamb. Then, and probably not until then, will this prophecy be fulfilled. "And I heard, as it were, the voice of a great multitude, as the sound of many waters and as the sound of mighty thunderings, saying, 'Alleluia! For the Lord God Omnipotent reigns! Let us be glad and rejoice and give Him glory, for the marriage of the Lamb has come, and His wife has made herself ready' (Revelation 19:6-7; NKJ).

BIBLIOGRAPHY

Bainton, Roland H. *Here I Stand: A Life of Martin Luther*. New York: New American Library, 1978.

Brecht, Martin. *Martin Luther: His Road to Reformation*. Trans. James L. Schaaf. Philadelphia: Fortress Press, 1985.

Bryant, Arthur. *Protestant Island*. London: Collins, 1967.

Cambridge History of English Literature. Volumes II & III. New York: Macmillan, 1933.

Chaucer, Geoffrey. *The Canterbury Tales*. Trans. Neville Coghill. Penguin, 1952.

Grimm, Harold J. *The Reformation Era*. New York: Macmillan, 1954.

Horton, Rod W. *Backgrounds of American Literary Thought*. Englewood, NJ: Prentice-Hall, 1974.

Lilje, Hanns. *Martin Luther*. Bonn: Inter Nations, 1983.

Martin Luther: Selections from his Writings. E. John Dillenberger. Garden City, NY: Anchor Books, 1961.

Trevelyan, G. M. *English Social History*. Longmans: 1948.

Youings, Joyce. *Sixteenth-Century England*. Allen Lane, 1984.

www.ingramcontent.com/pod-product-compliance
Lightning Source LLC
Chambersburg PA
CBHW032127090426
42743CB00007B/500